LONDON'S
HIDDEN
RIVERS

LONDON'S HIDDEN RIVERS

A walker's guide to the
subterranean waterways of London

Written & illustrated by
DAVID FATHERS

FRANCES
LINCOLN

The Quarto Group
6 Blundell Street
London N7 9BH
United Kingdom

ISBN: 978-0-7112-3554-0

Printed and bound in China

9 8 7 6 5 4 3

Disclaimer

*The routes of the hidden streams displayed in this book are based upon research using
available historical and current maps, reference books and upon personal observations.
Occasionally the author has found contradictions in the route a stream may take. The
ones featured in this book are based upon the most reliable sources available. However,
given that these waterways are hidden from view, their precise locations cannot always
be guaranteed and these maps should not be relied upon for any purposes of insurance,
planning or legal usage.*

MIX
Paper from
responsible sources
FSC® C008047

*Contour map: Contains OS data © Crown
copyright and database right 2016*

LONDON'S HIDDEN RIVERS
CONTENTS

Lee Navigation

N

E

Above:
Old Father Thames outside Hammersmith & Fulham Town Hall.

Opposite page:
Top: 1862: The River Fleet bursts into the Underground railway embankment.
Right: Two ceramic spa water flasks.
Far right: Hollowed-out elm boughs used as water pipes.

INTRODUCTION

A dropped match or a spark was probably the cause of the River Fleet exploding in 1846. It badly damaged a steamer close to the sluice gate on the Thames at Blackfriars and flooded many adjacent cellars in the Farringdon area. An accumulation of methane and other inflammable gases within the badly managed Fleet sewer had ignited with dire consequences.

Sixteen years later engineers rerouted the Fleet south of King's Cross to make way for the world's first underground railway. The Fleet, which had already been press-ganged into sewer duties, was being moved again. In 1862, during a very heavy rainstorm, the Fleet burst out of its confinement and onto the newly prepared railway embankment, flooding it up to a depth of 4m. It took weeks to clear and repair the damage. Once again the river had wreaked its revenge.

How had it come to this? In medieval London, rivers were often seen not only as a source of water for drinking, cleaning and powering mills, but also as a disposal facility. Tanners, slaughterhouses and brewers would all throw discarded offcuts, gore and dregs into the streams. Along with human waste and dead animals these rivers had become rancid, open sewers. In 1357, during the reign of Edward III, legislation was passed in an attempt to keep the waterways clean and unclogged. It had a limited effect.

A land of wells

By the seventeenth century, the quality of drinking water taken from the rivers had declined so far in London that many now sought water supplies from further afield. Companies such as the Hampstead Water Company began to pipe water from the Fleet on Hampstead Heath into the City of London in hollowed-out elm boughs. The New River Company built a canal to bring spring water into Islington from Hertfordshire.

Alternatively, some people were travelling out to the sources of the Thames tributaries to 'take the waters' at the newly 'discovered' spas and wells. They were drawn by the advertised medicinal and healing qualities of the waters. By the mid-eighteenth century it had become very fashionable to drink the waters and be seen at the new spas.

In Hampstead, north London, the spas were supplying not only the mineral waters but also entertainment, food and dancing. Similar establishments were being founded all around London: in places like Streatham, Acton, Sydenham and Kilburn. For those not wishing to travel so far out of London, at least eight spas and wells could be found around the King's Cross area.

The Great Stink

By 1801, the population of London stood at just over one million. Sixty years later this figure had trebled. The process of industrialisation, which had begun in the eighteenth century, was drawing ever more workers and their families into the capital, placing an even greater demand on water supplies and sewage removal.

The rivers became ever more putrid, toxic and disease-ridden. The only solution was to bury them. Incrementally, most central London tributaries of the Thames were covered over, buried and largely forgotten about. Eventually, this process of culverting would reach as far as the source. By the mid-nineteenth century, many of London's villages that had originally established themselves on a stream or a well had merged and, with the assistance of the railways, began forming into suburbs.

Despite the massive growth of London's population, the system of sewage disposal had not kept pace. Most of Londoners' human ordure was disposed of into cesspits, which were then cleared by sewage removal people, known as 'nightmen' (for they usually worked under the cover of darkness, carrying the dung away in horse-drawn carts). This was a system that had been in place for hundreds of years but was wholly unsuitable for an ever-burgeoning metropolis.

In 1849, 49,000 Londoners died in a cholera outbreak and, following the discovery by Dr John Snow that the disease was not airborne, as had been popularly thought, but was carried by contaminated water, the Metropolitan Board of Works was established by an Act of Parliament in 1856. Its prime objective was to create a network of interconnected sewer pipes for the capital. Joseph Bazalgette, appointed chief engineer, was tasked with bringing this mammoth project into existence. Streets were excavated and houses demolished, all to build a new sewage grid. London's now-subterranean rivers were press-ganged into this network.

Gone but not forgotten

Rivers have often acted as natural boundaries between countries, counties and boroughs. In parts of London this is still the case. Though the rivers can no longer be seen, they still act as borders.

The Royal Borough of Kensington & Chelsea has several of its borders defined by culverted rivers. Its eastern border with Westminster is defined, in part, by the River Westbourne and its western border, with the London Borough of Hammersmith & Fulham, is almost entirely denoted by Counter's Creek. In Kensal Green Cemetery, the cast-iron boundary markers are still visible

between the gravestones. The counties of Surrey and Kent used to have their border defined, close to the Thames, by the Earl's Sluice, until they were redrawn in 1899.

Often London street names commemorate and mark hidden rivers. Just the reference to a 'brook' or a 'bourne' is usually a good indicator of a subterranean river nearby: for example, Upbrook Mews, Westbourne Terrace, Ashbourne Road or Pont Street. Counter's Creek, not blessed with streets named after the watercourse, does have the oblique Clearwater Terrace.

On Hampstead Heath, the 300-year-old man-made ponds, filled by the River Fleet, now present a potential risk of overflowing and flooding the areas immediately to the south. Remedial work has been undertaken to reduce this threat by raising the heights of the dams.

In July 2007, following a heavy rainstorm and despite the efforts of the local pumping station, Falcon Brook erupted out of its subterranean pipe and flooded an area of Battersea, damaging homes and businesses. The hidden rivers of London, though buried, still like to remind us that they exist.

Far left: The former parish boundary marker that once stood on a bridge over the Earl's Sluice in Deptford.
Left: A manhole cover over the River Falcon in Streatham.
Above: Inside the Ranelagh Sewer, Chelsea.
Right: The Holborn Viaduct over Farringdon Street with the subterranean River Fleet flowing below.

Locating a hidden river

In certain parts of London, finding a subterranean river is not that difficult. Northcote Road, Battersea, under which Falcon Brook

Lothbury, outside the Wren church St Margaret Lothbury. The red line denotes the horizontal. The blue line indicates the route of the subterranean Walbrook.

flows, is a classic example of a steep river valley. The streets to the east and the west of the road drop steeply towards it. Parts of King's Cross Road are similar as the valley bottom indicates the River Fleet below.

Tracking the River Walbrook in the City of London can be much harder. Over the centuries, as buildings were demolished, the rubble was not always removed but simply built upon. The valley that the Walbrook had formed has been filled in. Twenty-first-century building techniques do not assist either, as engineers have the power to transform landscapes and remove any trace of

natural indentations. However, there are clues on certain streets. On Lothbury, for example, just north of the Bank of England, follow the horizontal lines close to the base of St Margaret Lothbury and notice the subtle dip in the pavement and the street *(see illustration left)* where the Walbrook flows below.

On the former marshland, south of the Thames, traces of the culverted rivers are almost impossible to see with the naked eye. This lowland, part of which was once submerged beneath a broader Thames, has very few natural undulations. The buried streams (namely the Earl's Sluice and the River Neckinger) that cross this area are drainage ditches and may well have been man-made or at least re-navigated by man. The Rivers Effra and Peck also flow beneath this area, although hardly scarring the landscape. However, in places further south on the Dulwich and Sydenham Hills, as these streams descend off the slopes, their routes are more discernible and even occasionally make appearances in the form of ponds.

A street sloping down to Northcote Road, Battersea.

Using this book

This book features twelve hidden rivers of London and describes over 125km (75 miles) of walks, the course of each subterranean waterway. Each chapter is designed to be walked from source to the Thames (or, in the case of the Hackney Brook, to the Lee Navigation). They could, of course, easily be walked in reverse: from Thames to the source. The route is shown by a dotted red line. In certain places some thoroughfares are closed at given times. Alternative routes are marked.

Each chapter's introduction includes the distance covered for the entire walk. If you only plan to walk a section of a river, each double page denotes the length covered on those pages in the bottom right-hand corner.

All Underground and railway stations adjacent to the walks are clearly marked throughout the book.

Subterranean river		FP	*Footpath/pedestrianised area*
Exposed river			*Railway station*
• • • • • *The route*			*Underground station*
• • • • • *Alternative route*			*Overground station*
Steps			*Clipper pier*

STAMFORD BROOK

Complete walk: From Park Royal 9.1km
Complete walk: From Acton Main Line 6.6km (page 16)

The subterranean rivers that flow under Acton, Chiswick and Hammersmith comprise three streams: East and West Stamford Brook (eastern and central arms) and Bollo Brook (western arm). Only once the three merge, close to Ravenscourt Park in Hammersmith, does the waterway become known as Stamford Brook.

Park Royal Underground

The river's name has probably evolved from the Saxon word *steanford*, meaning a 'stone ford'. This was a safe crossing place on the Roman road along what is now Bath Road in Chiswick.

Despite the name of this river, there is no connection whatsoever with Stamford Bridge, the former crossing and football ground on Counter's Creek, some 3km to the east. Bollo Brook forms part of the boundary between the London Boroughs of Hounslow and Hammersmith & Fulham.

The streams flow under what is largely late-nineteenth- and twentieth-century residential areas, with some office and industrial zones along the routes too. Until the late 1920s, Stamford Brook formed a 260m-long open creek where it entered the River Thames, and at high water barges could enter the inlet to unload and load cargo. A whole infrastructure of wharves and warehouses for the shipping of goods by water was established. These have all been demolished and replaced with a town hall and a riverside park.

Most rivers of central London were covered over by the mid-nineteenth century. The areas of Acton, Chiswick and Hammersmith developed later as residential and industrial areas and consequently Stamford Brook was not fully covered over until the early twentieth century.

1 Park Royal station

The first station here was built in 1903 to serve the Royal Agricultural Society's Park Royal showgrounds just to the north. A new permanent Piccadilly line station was opened in 1936 *(right)* and was then named 'Park Royal (Hanger Hill)'. The Art Deco brick structure is a series of simple interlocking geometric shapes. Its design was directed by the Underground's chief architect, Charles Holden.

West Acton Underground

Noel Road

Monks Drive

Queen's Drive

Links Road

Vale Lane

Ashbourne Road

Audley Rd

Corringway

Boileau Rd

HANGER HILL

Heathcroft

Right: For a short stretch, Bollo Brook is an open stream, though not accessible to the public.

3 Passmore Edwards Cottage Hospital, Acton

The philanthropist John Passmore Edwards, along with the Rothschild family, contributed to the establishment of this cottage hospital *(right)*, which opened in 1898. Initially, residents of Acton and the impoverished were admitted free of charge and were treated by volunteer doctors. During the twentieth century the hospital expanded to include seventy-two beds and was absorbed into the NHS in 1948. It finally closed as a hospital in 2001.

4 Bollo Brook

The stream that rises on Ashbourne Road, Hanger Hill, is known as Bollo Brook. Once it is joined by two other tributary streams near Ravenscourt Park, it becomes Stamford Brook. Confusingly, however, the three streams collectively are known as Stamford Brook.

Below: A collection of London Transport signposts and a 1930s tram at the Museum Depot.

5 London Transport Museum Depot

This museum is the environmentally controlled store-room and conservation area for the London Transport Museum based in Covent Garden. Over 370,000 items are held here, including vintage Tube trains, buses, taxis, posters, signs, maps, ephemera and uniforms. Its role is to explain and conserve the transport history of London. Access to the Museum Depot is usually by booking a themed guided tour or attending one of the open days.

2 Hanger Hill Garden Estate

The subterranean Bollo Brook passes under a very striking mock-Tudor estate. Two- and three-storey blocks of half-timbered flats and semi-detached houses of the Hanger Hill Garden Estate *(left)* sit in well-tended, spacious landscaped gardens. They were designed by Douglas Smith & Barley and constructed in 1928–36. Good transport access via West Acton and North Ealing Underground stations have made the estate a very desirable location to live in. In this conservation zone, refuse trucks are not allowed to use the front roads but must use the service lanes to empty the wheelie bins.

Walking these pages: 4.2km

①

Acton Town Underground

1 Acton Town station

This was built in 1932 for London Transport, one of architect Charles Holden's first designs for the Piccadilly line extension. The large rectangular brick, concrete and glass booking hall sits over the tracks below. It is now a Grade II listed building. The Tube line closely follows the path of Bollo Brook as far as Hammersmith.

Right: Bollo Bridge Road, once the site of a crossing over the stream.

Bollo Bridge Rd

Bollo Lane

2 Gunnersbury Triangle Nature Reserve

This 2.6-hectare nature reserve, run by the London Wildlife Trust, is surrounded on all three sides by railway tracks. Allotments once occupied part of the land but these closed in the 1940s and so the area was able to develop, unhindered by Man, for many decades. It opened as a nature reserve in 1985, following a campaign to protect the land from developers. The reserve now has a wildlife population including birds, insects, amphibians and plants. The entrance to the reserve is on Bollo Lane and admission is free. The London Wildlife Trust is a charity dedicated to the protection of the capital's wild spaces and wildlife.

4 Bedford Park

Bedford Park was the world's first garden suburb. Ten hectares of land were acquired by Jonathan Carr in 1875, largely because of its proximity to the new Turnham Green station and the existing mature trees within the estate. In 1877, Carr appointed Richard Norman Shaw chief architect for the estate. Shaw's vision was for a quiet, leafy suburb with facilities such as a club, a church and even a school of art. However, despite the initial desirability of the area in the 1880s, it went into decline and by the 1950s many houses were in a poor state of repair with a few being demolished. By 1968, following the action of a few locals to establish the Bedford Park Society, the 356 houses became Grade II listed and a conservation area was established.

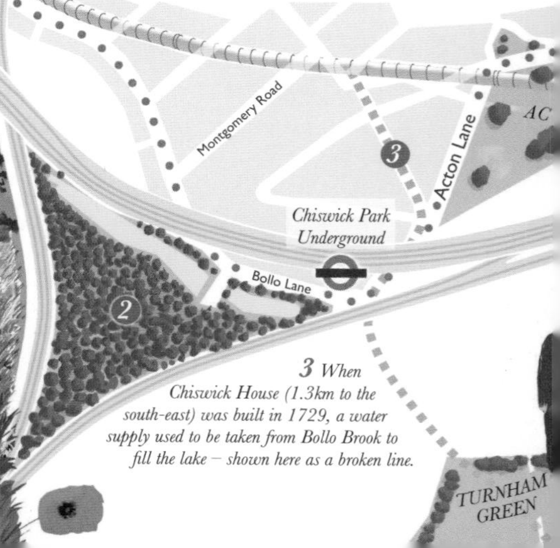

Montgomery Road

Acton Lane

AC

③

Chiswick Park Underground

Bollo Lane

②

3 When

Chiswick House (1.3km to the south-east) was built in 1729, a water supply used to be taken from Bollo Brook to fill the lake – shown here as a broken line.

TURNHAM GREEN

6 Stamford Brook Underground station

Stamford Brook Underground station is one of a small number of stations named after London's hidden rivers. Kilburn and Bayswater stations are named after former titles of the River Westbourne. Holborn (Old Bourne) Underground station is also a good candidate for a station named after a hidden river. The river ran eastwards from a point close to the station to join the River Fleet in Farringdon. However, the stream has long since been rerouted and dried up.

Page 17

Stamford Brook Road

STAMFORD BROOK COMMON

⑦

Page 18

7 Brook House, home of Pissarro (see page 18).

STAMFORD BROOK

⑥

Stamford Brook Underground

Bath Road

④ *Turnham Green Underground*

Below left: Soldiers loyal to King Charles I muster on Turnham Green in 1642 to face troops of Cromwell's army (below right).

South Parade

⑤

CHISWICK COMMON

...MON

5 Battle of Turnham Green

In late October 1642, during the English Civil War, Charles I and his Royalist army had taken Banbury and continued along the Thames Valley with the hope of recapturing the capital. By mid-November, Oliver Cromwell's Parliamentarian army, under the command of the Earl of Essex, lined up a 24,000-strong force, many of whom were untrained civilians, along the eastern edge of Turnham Green. (The Green stretched much further north and included what is now Acton and Chiswick Commons.) The Royalists arrived with only 13,000 troops. Lacking man-power and the support of Londoners, they decided not to attack first. Some skirmishes did break out between the lines, resulting in a few deaths. The confrontation was largely a stand-off, causing the Royalists to retreat back to Oxford for the winter.

Walking these pages: 3.3km

1 Acton laundries

The rapid expansion of middle-class areas such as Kensington and Notting Hill in the 1860s and the ready supply of soft water from Stamford Brook led to the development of small hand laundries being set up close to what is now Steyne Road. A more mechanised, large-scale laundry appeared with the arrival of the Empire Steam Laundry in 1873. By 1900, Acton was the largest laundry town in the UK, with nearly 3,000 people employed in the business. This consisted largely of women whose husbands worked in the nearby brickworks.

Acton Wells

Just to the north-east of where Stamford Brook rises were once located three spas. Although now buried under railway lines and a train depot, they still feed into the brook. In its day, the best known of these spas was Acton Wells. By the early eighteenth century, drinking the calcium carbonated waters had become very fashionable, so much so that it was bottled and sold in London.

Top: The Acton Wells Assembly Rooms.
Above: The first Waitrose store.

2 Waite, Rose & Taylor

Wallace Waite became an apprentice grocer aged thirteen. In 1904, nine years later, he teamed up with Arthur Rose and David Taylor to establish a grocery outlet in a new parade of shops at 263 High Street, Acton. The manager, Taylor, left the business a few years later, leaving Waite and Rose to form a limited company, Waitrose. By 1937 it had ten stores before being taken over by the John Lewis Partnership. Today, the supermarket chain has over 350 stores across the UK.

4&5 Beneath manhole covers on Avenue Road and Mansell Road the West Stamford Brook can be heard flowing.

Left: A pavement plaque locating the first Waitrose.
Above: Berrymead Priory.

WENDELL PARK

6 The Wilkinson Sword Company

The Wilkinson Sword Company was typical of a new breed of manufacturers starting up in Acton in the early twentieth century. They moved on to the former brickworks site (which later became Southfield Playing Fields) in 1905. Here they produced swords, razors, typewriters and the Wilkinson touring motorcycles. During the First World War, Wilkinson manufactured over two million bayonets. In a very short space of time the area attracted many other motor and aero manufacturers including Renault, Bosch, Lucas and Napier & Sons.

Flanchford Road

Hartswood Road

Wendell Road

Warple Way

Cobbold Rd

Emlyn Road

Canham Road

FP

Hatfield Road

Stamford Brook Road

STAMFORD BROOK COMMON

Page 18

8 *The West Stamford Brook can sometimes be heard beneath the manhole cover (right) at the end of Warple Way, by the gates. The Warple was once a name for this section of West Stamford Brook.*

7 Acton Pumping Station

This is a set of six storm overflow tanks built on the line of West Stamford Brook. In the event of heavy rainfall, these tanks can hold 18,000m^3 of excess rainwater and sewage and prevent the flooding of local streets and houses. Once the surge has passed, the water and sewage is slowly released back into the system.

Below: One of the empty overflow tanks at Acton Pumping Station.

SOUTHFIELD PLAYING FIELDS

Above right: A Wilkinson Sword motorcycle.
Right: Bayonets manufactured by Wilkinson Sword Company during the First World War.

3 Berrymead Priory

From the mid-seventeenth century until the end of the twentieth, a mansion house stood on this site. Sitting within 4.6 hectares, the West Stamford Brook flowed through the grounds. Before the area was urbanised in the nineteenth century, the house had often been used as a country retreat. Despite its name (the title 'Priory' was a historical fantasy), it only acted as a religious house and boarding school between 1842 and 1850. Having passed through many owners, including the Conservative Party and Acton District Council, the final incarnation of Berrymead Priory was demolished in 1985.

Walking these pages: 5.0km

1 Lucien Pissarro and Brook House

Lucien Pissarro (1863–1944), the eldest son of the Danish-French impressionist painter Emile Pissarro, was born in Paris. Lucien was an impressionist painter like his father, specialising in landscapes and book illustration. He and his family finally settled in south-east England in 1890 and moved to Brook House on Stamford Brook Road twelve years later. The house is very close to the point where Bollo Brook and West Stamford Brook meet.

RAVENSCOURT PARK

Paddenswick Road

Goldhawk Rd

Ravenscourt Sq

Goldhawk Road

Page 17

Page 15

Stamford Brook Road

STAMFORD BROOK COMMON

Bath Road

*Below
(left to right):
Brook House; a sample
of Brook Type; and the former
moat in Ravenscourt Park.*

2 Ravenscourt Park

The medieval Paddenswick Manor was surrounded by a moat that was fed from Stamford Brook. The remains of the moat can be seen today as a pond within the park, though nothing remains of the manor house. Ravenscourt Park remained in private ownership until the 1880s and was nearly sold for property development until local householders saved the open space. It was transferred to the Metropolitan Board of Works, which developed it as 13 hectares of public park.

BEN JONSON'S SONGS. SELECTION from THE PLAYS, MASQUES, & POEMS, WITH THE EARLIEST KNOWN MUSIC OF CERTAIN NUMBERS.

Brook Type

Inspired by William Morris's Kelmscott Press (located just to the west of Hammersmith Creek), Lucien Pissarro established the Eragny Press, first at his first home in Epping in 1894 and later at Brook House in Chiswick. Pissarro not only produced wood engravings and designs for the books, he created the font too. Brook Type was based on Vale Type, a font created by Charles Ricketts. The font was probably named after Brook House and the stream that flowed nearby. The Eragny Press produced thirty-two titles until its closure in 1914.

3 Hammersmith Town Hall

Hammersmith Town Hall was built directly above the line of Stamford Brook in 1939, not long after the stream had been covered over. The brick and stone structure is the administrative headquarters for the London Borough of Hammersmith & Fulham. At the southern end of the building, overlooking Furnivall Park and the Thames, are two wide stone stairways leading down to street level. Each of these stairways is decorated with a representation of Old Father Thames. This is a reference back to a time when the area was dependent upon the Thames (and the lower end of Stamford Brook) for much of its trade.

Above: Hammersmith Town Hall.
Right: Old Father Thames.

4 Hammersmith Creek

The mouth of Stamford Brook was once known as Hammersmith Creek. It was a tidal inlet that at high tide allowed barges to reach as far as King Street. With surrounding wharves and warehouses the area became very industrialised and earned the name Little Wapping, after the much bigger docks to the east. The Creek closed in 1929 and was later culverted. Furnivall Gardens, an open green space, was created in 1951 on what was the site of the old creek and wharf building. The gardens are named after Dr Frederick Furnivall, the co-founder of the Oxford English Dictionary.

Above: A Thames barge at Hammersmith Creek.
Below: The Stamford Brook outfall into the Thames.

5 The Dove

The Dove *(above)* is a seventeenth-century pub adjacent to the River Thames. Measuring just 1.3m × 2.4m, it is the smallest bar in the UK, according to Guinness World Records. It is believed that in this pub, in 1740, James Thomson wrote the words of the song 'Rule, Britannia!'

THE DOVE

Dalling Road

Ravenscourt Park Underground

King Street

Nigel Playfair Avenue

Great West Rd

FURNIVALL GARDENS

RIVER THAMES

Hammersmith Bridge

Walking these pages: 1.6km

N

COUNTER'S CREEK

Complete walk 9.6km

This has to be one of London's least known and least loved hidden rivers. Even though it flows through some of the most affluent areas of London, it is trampled under roads and railways and is less well known than some of its neighbouring streams, such as the Fleet.

Counter's Creek acts as the boundary between the London Boroughs of Hammersmith & Fulham and Kensington & Chelsea. It has two of London's 'Magnificent Seven' cemeteries – Kensal Green and Brompton – on its banks. Two large auditoria once sat adjacent to the stream: White City and Earls Court and a third, Olympia, is still operational today. The football ground of Chelsea FC, Stamford Bridge, is also situated by the creek.

The name of the stream hails from a bridge, Contessebrugge, that once straddled the creek and was named after a local countess, Matilda. There are no streets named after the stream, except for the obliquely named Clearwater Terrace in Holland Park.

Due to the river's large watershed, which includes Camden and Brent, it can pose a major flooding threat. Despite additional storm sewers having been built nearby, flash storms can still flood basements in the area.

1 Kensal Green Cemetery

With London's population growing in the early nineteenth century, the need for more burial space increased. Kensal Green Cemetery opened in 1833 and became one of London's 'Magnificent Seven' burial sites. It was modelled on the Père Lachaise Cemetery in Paris. Around a quarter of a million bodies are interred within the largely gothic-styled catacombs, colonnades and graves. The neoclassical Anglican and Dissenters' Chapels are both listed buildings, along with many of the monuments. Notables buried within the 29-hectare cemetery include the Victorian master engineers Isambard Kingdom Brunel and his son Marc, the author Wilkie Collins, the playwright Harold Pinter and the first computer scientist, Charles Babbage.

A crematorium was built on the western side of Kensal Green Cemetery. Freddie Mercury and Ingrid Bergman were cremated here. Counter's Creek rises within Kensal Green Cemetery close to an unmarked well. The route is marked by borough boundary markers as the river forms the border between the boroughs of Hammersmith & Fulham and Kensington & Chelsea.

Kensal Green station

West Gate

Harrow Road

Alma Pl

alternative footpath

Left: An ornate gothic grave.

Scrubs Lane

There is a pedestrian gate in the wall on Scrubs Lane. Check at the West Gate for opening times. Otherwise use the main footpath shown.

Above: The crematorium gardens are located within a valley adjacent to a boundary wall. This is possibly a tributary of Counter's Creek.

crematorium

Grand Union Canal

Grand Union Canal

This 220km waterway, formerly known as the Grand Junction Canal, was built between 1793 and 1805 to connect the Midlands to London and the Thames. Horse-drawn barges hauled raw materials into and out of the rapidly expanding capital. There is a gate in the wall of Kensal Green Cemetery that once allowed coffins to be brought in by barge.

2 White City

Imre Kiralfy, a Hungarian showman, who in the late-nineteenth century had worked on popular entertainments such as 'Buffalo Bill' Cody's Wild West Show at Earls Court, was commissioned to create the Franco–British Exhibition in 1908. On a site north of Shepherd's Bush, Kiralfy's team created stucco pavilions (the White City) displaying exhibitions of industry and art surrounded by waterways, lagoons and landscaped gardens. For the 100,000 paying visitors per day there were also fairground rides, circus shows and even fabricated Celtic and Senegalese villages, complete with 'native' occupants. In the same year, the fourth Olympic Games track and field events were held in the White City Stadium, adjacent to Kiralfy's extravaganza. The games became famous for the moment when Italian marathon runner Dorando Pietri was assisted across the finish line and was disqualified. Kiralfy created more shows at White City up until the First World War. Following the war, the exhibitions and entertainments were not as popular. In 1926 the White City Stadium became a greyhound track, which lasted until 1983, before becoming the BBC Media Village. Virtually nothing, except a few street names, remain of this once extremely popular Edwardian entertainment centre.

Counter's Creek

3 The Westway

The Westway is an elevated dual carriageway, opened in 1970 to relieve traffic congestion at Shepherd's Bush. It was part of a huge plan to build motorways across and around London. Much of the scheme was abandoned due to costs and opposition.

Latimer Road Underground

Highlever Road

Oxford Gardens

Freston Road

Brewster Gardens

Dalgarno Gdns

'TTLE WORMWOOD SCRUBS

Mitre Way

Scrubs Lane

WORMWOOD SCRUBS

Wood Lane

3

Left to right: Marathon runner Dorando Pietri is assisted across the line in the 1908 Olympics; postcard views of White City and the stadium. Below: The location of the former stadium.

2

The Lagoons, White City, London 1908

Walking these pages: 3.3km

White City Underground

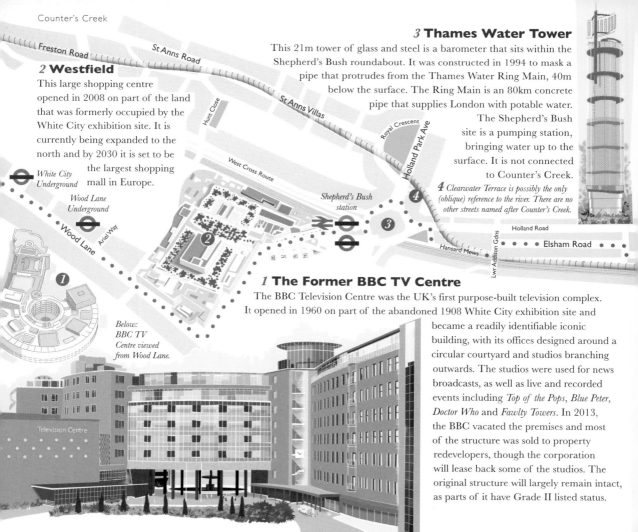

Counter's Creek

Freston Road

St Anns Road

2 **Westfield**

This large shopping centre opened in 2008 on part of the land that was formerly occupied by the White City exhibition site. It is currently being expanded to the north and by 2030 it is set to be the largest shopping mall in Europe.

White City Underground

Wood Lane Underground

Wood Lane

Arial Way

Hunt Close

West Cross Route

St Anns Villas

Royal Crescent

Holland Park Ave

Shepherd's Bush station

3 **Thames Water Tower**

This 21m tower of glass and steel is a barometer that sits within the Shepherd's Bush roundabout. It was constructed in 1994 to mask a pipe that protrudes from the Thames Water Ring Main, 40m below the surface. The Ring Main is an 80km concrete pipe that supplies London with potable water.

The Shepherd's Bush site is a pumping station, bringing water up to the surface. It is not connected to Counter's Creek.

4 Clearwater Terrace is possibly the only (oblique) reference to the river. There are no other streets named after Counter's Creek.

Hansard Mews

Lwr Addison Gdns

Holland Road

Elsham Road

1 **The Former BBC TV Centre**

The BBC Television Centre was the UK's first purpose-built television complex. It opened in 1960 on part of the abandoned 1908 White City exhibition site and became a readily identifiable iconic building, with its offices designed around a circular courtyard and studios branching outwards. The studios were used for news broadcasts, as well as live and recorded events including *Top of the Pops*, *Blue Peter*, *Doctor Who* and *Fawlty Towers*. In 2013, the BBC vacated the premises and most of the structure was sold to property redevelopers, though the corporation will lease back some of the studios. The original structure will largely remain intact, as parts of it have Grade II listed status.

Below: BBC TV Centre viewed from Wood Lane.

Television Centre

Left: A fifteenth century stone bridge once crossed Counter's Creek.

5 The Countess' Bridge

Around 1420, a bridge was built over Counter's Creek, close to where Kensington Olympia station is now. It was named the 'Contessebrugge', after Countess Matilda of Oxford, whose family held the local manor and possibly paid for its construction. It was a corruption of the bridge's name that gave the stream its title.

8 Earls Court

The first Earls Court exhibition and events venue opened in 1887, Buffalo Bill's Wild West Show being one of the first popular events to appear here. The centre was rebuilt in 1937 with an Art Deco frontage. The structure, the largest in Europe at the time, was built over the District line, using sixty reinforced concrete frames. It became a regular venue for The Motor Show. Like its rival exhibition hall Olympia, it has hosted numerous rock gigs, such as David Bowie, Pink Floyd and Muse. In 2014, the owners closed Earls Court and work started to redevelop the area into residential and retail space.

Earls Court Underground

Above: The main entrance to the former exhibition hall of Earls Court. Below: The Kensington Canal basin, as it would have looked in the 1830s.

Kensington (Olympia) station

6 Olympia

Olympia is a popular exhibition space, renowned for hosting the Ideal Home Exhibition. Its 52m arched iron roof, was delivered in sections by railway from Derby to the adjacent station. It opened to the public in 1886. Several new halls, including the modernist-styled Empire Hall, now Olympia Two *(featured left)*, have been added. During both World Wars it served as a German civilian internment camp. Today it still hosts major exhibitions, music concerts and boxing matches.

7 Kensington Canal

In the late 1820s, the lower 3km of Counter's Creek was canalised to a width of 30m. The canal was created to bring vital commodities such as coal and building materials to west London. A canal basin was created adjacent to what is now Olympia, complete with a lock. However, no lock was constructed at the southern end of the canal, which was at the mercy of the tides. Consequently, the business venture failed financially and the canal was bought by the West London Railway Company. In 1859, they filled in the canal, culverted the creek and laid railway lines above it.

Walking these pages: 3.9km

1 Brompton Cemetery

This, the second of the 'Magnificent Seven' cemeteries to sit on the banks of Counter's Creek (see page 20), opened in 1840. The site had previously been a market garden. The 16-hectare cemetery was founded by the architect and entrepreneur Stephen Geary. The site, designed by Benjamin Baud, was very formally laid out, with inspiration taken from cathedral design: a long 'nave', planted with lime trees, runs towards the 'altar' – the domed Anglican chapel. Long colonnades run either side of the central path, beneath which are located the catacombs. Following the 1850 Metropolitan Interments Act, the cemetery was nationalised and is now under the care of the Royal Parks. All of the structures and some mausoleums are now Grade II listed. Among the 200,000 buried here are the founder of Cunard Line Sir Samuel Cunard, the suffragette Emily Pankhurst and the physician Dr John Snow.

Old Brompton Road

Fulham Road

West Brompton station

Below: The eastern side of the colonnades (with the catacombs beneath). Right: the Anglican chapel.

2 Chelsea FC

The Premier League football team was founded in 1905 on the Fulham (western) side of Counter's Creek and played on what was the Stamford Bridge athletics ground. As Fulham Football Club had already been founded, they adopted the name of the neighbouring borough, Chelsea.

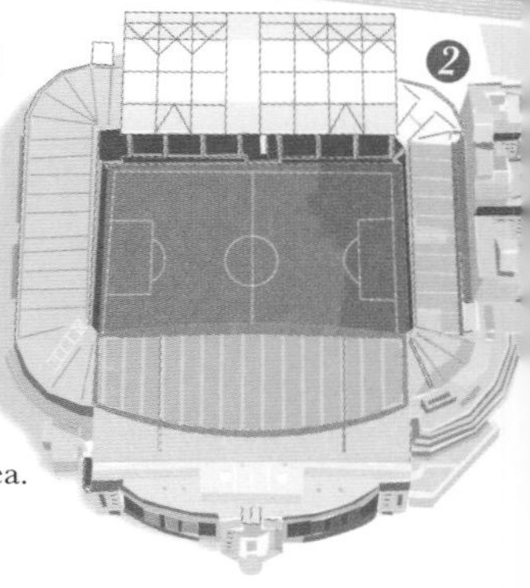

4 Lots Road Power Station

This former electricity-generating power station was created to supply power to the Brompton and Piccadilly Circus Railway (now part of the Piccadilly line). It opened in 1905 on the site of the Cremorne Pleasure Gardens. It would eventually supply power to the entire London Underground network. Originally, the power station had four chimneys, though this was reduced to two in the 1960s. The plant closed in 2002 and is currently being converted into residential and retail units.

Above: The view south, from King's Road bridge, of the railway track. Counter's Creek is buried below.

5 Chelsea Creek

Chelsea Creek is the only remaining section of the Kensington Canal. It was used by coal barges to supply Lots Road Power Station and the Imperial Gas Works.

Follow the Thames Path signposts to the river

Counter's Creek

RIVER THAMES

King's Road

Lots Road

P · Wandon Road ·

3 Sandyford Bridge

Before the bridge over Counter's Creek existed at Fulham Road there was a ford through a sandy riverbed. The name has evolved over the centuries into 'Stamford Bridge'. It is not related to Stamford Brook located further west of here.

6 Chelsea Harbour

Chelsea Harbour is a waterside complex of luxury residential apartments, shops, offices and a hotel. Despite its name it is located in the borough of Hammersmith & Fulham. It opened in 1989. Much of the development is structured around a marina, which was created in the nineteenth century as dock for railway transshipment. Today, it is stocked with expensive super-yachts. The Belvedere Tower, which dominates the site, is twenty-one storeys high (76m). It is topped off with a golden sphere that rises and falls with the tidal river.

Imperial Wharf station

Walking these pages: 2.4km

RIVER WESTBOURNE

Complete walk 14.5km

The River Westbourne is one of three hidden rivers in London that rise on Hampstead Heath and flow south to join the Thames. John Constable depicted the source of the river in his painting *Branch Hill Pond* in 1828 *(right)*. Although much has changed, the small valley to the west of the Heath is still wild and verdant. The Westbourne flows almost southerly and is nearly all subterranean until it reaches the Thames. It used to feed the Serpentine lake, until it became too polluted and had to be rerouted.

Despite being driven underground over 160 years ago, the River Westbourne was, and still is, known by other names in places along its length: the Kilburn, the Bayswater and the Ranelagh. The Westbourne (or the western brook) was known as such in the area around Paddington. Street names still celebrate the river's presence in the area, including Westbourne Grove, Westbourne Terrace, as well as another dozen other Westbourne prefixes.

One striking theme that unites this river along its route is music. From the house where Paul Robeson lived, the studios where a legendary 1960s pop band recorded a famously unsuccessful demo, the BBC's renowned recording studios in Maida Vale, the location where the star of *The Wizard of Oz* tragically died, and finally the gardens where a very young Mozart performed.

Opposite page, clockwise from top right: View of West End Lane, c.1900; Harmsworth plaque in Pandora Road; Sir Adrian Boult; a detail of Spedan Close housing; stream cover on Redington Gardens; a contemporary view of Branch Hill valley, and Branch Hill Pond *(1828) by John Constable.*

⊖ *Hampstead Underground*

1 West Heath

West Heath is a spur of Hampstead Heath, divided by the road connecting Golders Green to Hampstead and, like the main Heath, was largely sandy earth covered with gorse. Until the mid-1800s the area was quite treeless. During the nineteenth century, the landowner Sir Thomas Maryon Wilson *(see page 51)* decided to extract sand for building work and plant trees. It resulted in the landscape we see today.

2 Branch Hill

At the lowest tip of West Heath is a grassy, tree-lined bowl, from which the River Westbourne, or Kilburn as it is often referred to here, rises. Rainwater filtering through the Bagshot Sands emerges on Branch Hill, where it meets a strata of non-porous Claygate Beds. This is usually a quiet part of the Heath, quite detached from the main Heath to the east.

3 Paul Robeson

In 1928, the singer and actor Paul Robeson *(left)* appeared in the musical *Show Boat* at the Theatre Royal, Drury Lane, playing the part of Joe. The following year he bought a house on Branch Hill, Hampstead. During his residency here, he took the lead role in *Othello*, playing opposite Peggy Ashcroft.

5 Outside Oak Tree House, where the footpath emerges into Redington Gardens, there is a drain cover. The Westbourne can sometimes be heard flowing below.

ENGLISH HERITAGE
PAUL ROBESON
1898-1976
Singer and Actor
lived here
1929-1930

7 West End

This 'West End' was once a small quiet hamlet, set in parkland, to the west of Hampstead, focused around the small green that remains today. A small thoroughfare, called West End Lane, still meanders gently up the hill, running from Kilburn High Road to Finchley Road, passing through West End. Originally, it ran as far as Hampstead. When the railways arrived between 1857 and 1879, the engineers created railway cuttings that ran east–west under West End Lane. The district expanded rapidly and the hamlet became a thriving commuter suburb for professionals and working class alike. One of the stations was named West Hampstead, to avoid confusion with the other emerging West End in central London.

River Westbourne

8 Alfred Harmsworth

The journalist and newspaper proprietor Alfred Harmsworth (1865–1922) lived at the newly built 31 Pandora Road in 1888. Two years later he established the Pandora Publishing Company. He, along with his brothers, would later establish the best-selling newspapers the *Daily Mail* and the *Daily Mirror*.

4 Spedan Close

Once known as Branch Hill Estate, these former council houses, built by the London Borough of Camden in the late 1970s, are often referred to as the most expensive of their type ever built in the UK. With roof terraces and distinctive external spiral staircases *(right)*, they were far from the average social housing stock. In 2010 they became Grade II listed buildings.

6 The conductor Sir Adrian Boult, 1889–1983, (right) lived at 78 Marlborough Mansion on Cannon Hill from 1966 until 1977.

ALFRED HARMSWORTH
Viscount Northcliffe
1865 - 1922
Journalist and
Newspaper Proprietor
lived here

Walking these pages: 2.5km

1 Railway stations of West Hampstead

Prior to 1857, West Hampstead, or West End as it was then known, was a small hamlet to the north-west of the capital. In that year the Hampstead Junction Railway opened a station on West End Lane, followed eleven years later by the Midland line station opening just 100m away. A third station arrived in 1879. This would later become a stop on the Jubilee line, part of the Underground network. With fast, efficient access to central London, the area, now known as West Hampstead, expanded rapidly. In each case, during the construction of the railways, the River Westbourne was driven beneath the tracks.

Mr. Epstein,
We don't like
their sound and
guitar groups
are on their
way out

2 The Beatles rejected

On Broadhurst Gardens, just off West End Lane, sits a two-storey brick structure. This is currently used as rehearsal studios for the English National Opera. Over half a century ago it was used by Decca Records and it was here on New Year's Day 1962 that the then-unknown Beatles turned up to record fifteen demo tracks in the hope of securing a contract. Decca turned them down, stating that 'guitar groups are on their way out'.

3 The Moonlight Club

On the first floor of The Railway pub, a small jazz and rhythm 'n' blues venue was opened in 1961, named Klooks Kleek. It was here that many fledgling bands and artists performed, including the Rolling Stones, Cream, Jimi Hendrix, John Mayall, Stevie Wonder and Rod Stewart. The venue closed in 1970, but re-emerged later as the Moonlight Club. In April 1980, Joy Division played one of their final gigs here. The following month, the band's singer Ian Curtis committed suicide.

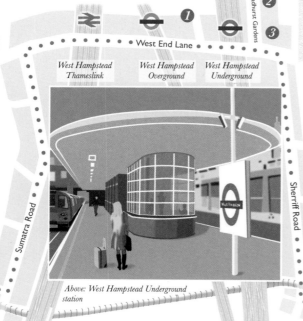

Above: West Hampstead Underground station

4 Right: The River Westbourne can sometimes be heard flowing under West End Lane. On the pavement just to the west of the former Bird in Hand pub is a modern rectangular aluminium manhole cover (marked here with an X).

5 Ebenezer Chapel

This small chapel was built in 1870 in memory of the Baptist preacher Thomas Creswick, who worked in the area of Kilburn and the surrounding district. A plaque that once featured on the front of the building stated that Creswick delivered his last sermon on a bridge close to this spot. The chapel is built within what was once the grounds of Kilburn Priory.

6 Kilburn Wells Spa

The spa was located within the gardens of The Bell Tavern on what was then known as Edgware Road. Located on this major thoroughfare, the spa became extremely popular in the 1750s with those wishing to 'take the waters'. The spa water contained magnesium and sodium sulphate and was described as milky in appearance with a bitter taste but was considered efficacious in the treatment of liver problems. A pub called The Old Bell still stands on Kilburn High Road today and a pavement plaque marks the site of the well.

Below: Kilburn High Road Overground

Upper left: Ebenezer Chapel. Lower left: The pavement plaque marking the location of Kilburn Wells Spa. Below: The former Kilburn Priory.

7 Kilburn Priory

Close to where a tributary joins the Westbourne, a priory was established around 1130 by a small group of nuns. This site had previously been occupied by a hermit. The priory became a point of refuge for pilgrims heading up Watling Way (now Kilburn High Road) to St Albans Cathedral. The establishment was dissolved in 1537 on the instructions of Henry VIII and the estate sold to the Prior of the Hospital of St John. Kilburn Priory is still remembered in several of the street names: Priory Road, Hermit Place and Abbey Road (the one immortalised by The Beatles).

Walking these pages: 2.8km

River Westbourne

1 St Augustine's Church

Kilburn is dominated by the soaring 77m spire of St Augustine's Church. The red brick structure, designed by the Gothic Revivalist architect J.L. Pearson, was consecrated in 1877. St Augustine's is probably Pearson's best-known church.

Some of his other church designs include Truro Cathedral and the Fitzrovia Chapel (once part of the now-demolished Middlesex Hospital, on Mortimer Street, W1). The supporting buttresses of the church are internal and the lavish ornate interior is of painted biblical scenes on the transept and below the gallery level. The altar and choir are rich with heavily carved details.

The Westbourne runs underground by the entrance of the church. St Augustine's Church is now Grade I listed.

Left: Paddington Recreation Ground. Bottom left: St Augustine's Church.

3 Paddington Recreation Ground

This very popular asset for the local community was first established in 1860 as a cricket ground provided by a local church. Twenty-eight years later it was opened to the public to provide 'recreation space'. The bandstand still remains from this era. Today, the much-redeveloped site includes an athletics track, tennis courts, a cricket pitch, two artificial grass pitches and a café. Sadly, the Westbourne does not make an appearance here but progresses below the ground.

2 Carlton Tavern

This exquisite pub, built in 1921 with partially tiled exterior and signage, was largely demolished, illegally, in 2015, when the developers had hoped to build flats on the site. Westminster City Council issued an enforcement order requiring the developers to rebuild the Carlton Tavern brick by brick.

Kilburn Park Rd · FP · Carlton Vale · Morshead Road · Essendine Road

Left: The Carlton Tavern

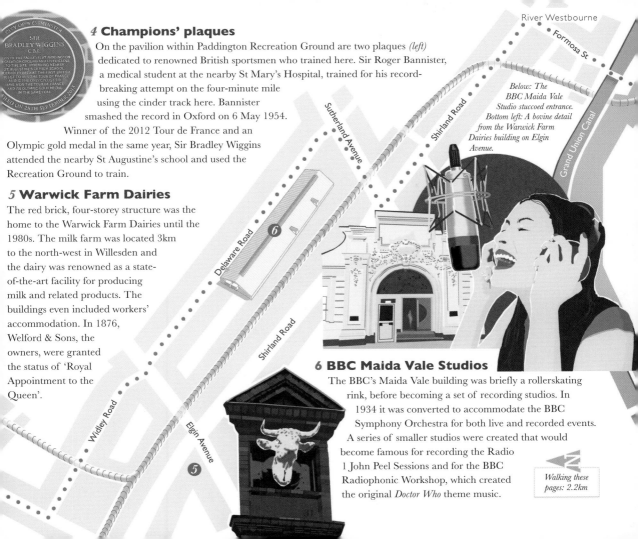

4 Champions' plaques

On the pavilion within Paddington Recreation Ground are two plaques *(left)* dedicated to renowned British sportsmen who trained here. Sir Roger Bannister, a medical student at the nearby St Mary's Hospital, trained for his record-breaking attempt on the four-minute mile using the cinder track here. Bannister smashed the record in Oxford on 6 May 1954.

Winner of the 2012 Tour de France and an Olympic gold medal in the same year, Sir Bradley Wiggins attended the nearby St Augustine's school and used the Recreation Ground to train.

5 Warwick Farm Dairies

The red brick, four-storey structure was the home to the Warwick Farm Dairies until the 1980s. The milk farm was located 3km to the north-west in Willesden and the dairy was renowned as a state-of-the-art facility for producing milk and related products. The buildings even included workers' accommodation. In 1876, Welford & Sons, the owners, were granted the status of 'Royal Appointment to the Queen'.

Below: The BBC Maida Vale Studio stuccoed entrance. Bottom left: A bovine detail from the Warwick Farm Dairies building on Elgin Avenue.

6 BBC Maida Vale Studios

The BBC's Maida Vale building was briefly a rollerskating rink, before becoming a set of recording studios. In 1934 it was converted to accommodate the BBC Symphony Orchestra for both live and recorded events. A series of smaller studios were created that would become famous for recording the Radio 1 John Peel Sessions and for the BBC Radiophonic Workshop, which created the original *Doctor Who* theme music.

Walking these pages: 2.2km

River Westbourne
1 **Little Venice**

In 1801, the Paddington Spur of the Grand Junction Canal was created to link London with the Midlands. The triangular section of water in Paddington was once a holding area for barges and the meeting point of the Grand Union and Regent's Canals. Today it is a quiet oasis known as Little Venice and the departure point for tourist barges heading off to Camden.

2 **Scars of transport**

The advance of transport development has left many huge scars on this area of west London. Starting in the late-eighteenth century, a spur of the Grand Junction Canal was cut from Harlington to Paddington. In 1838, Brunel's Great Western Railway devoured hectares of land to bring trains to and from western England and Wales. Finally, in 1970, the Westway was created to allow greater movement of motor traffic into and out of the capital. Many hundreds of houses were destroyed to make way for the elevated motorway.

*Top right: A view across Browning's Pool, Little Venice.
Right: A tower block within the Hallfield Estate.*

3 **Hallfield Estate**

The estate was designed by the Tecton Group in 1947, with the first batch of six- and ten-storey buildings being occupied in 1955. Following the break up of Tecton, the architects Lindsay Drake and Denis Lasdun fulfilled the project (Lasdun would go on to design the controversial National Theatre). The Hallfield Estate is deliberately set at 45 degrees to the surrounding stuccoed buildings and is complete with a school, shops and a laundry. The walkways are hidden behind distinctive abstract concrete screens *(left)* and the structures, despite their age, still have a contemporary appearance.

Little Venice
Paddington Spur
Formosa Street
Grand Union Canal
Delamere Ter. 300m detour to Little Venice
Senior Street
Bourne Terrace
WESTBOURNE GREEN
Harrow Road
A40 Westway
Lord Hill's Bridge
Royal Oak Underground
Porchester Road
Porchester Square
Bishop's Bridge Road
Gloucester Terrace
HALLFIELD ESTATE

4 A mews route

Once through the Hallfield Estate, the Westbourne runs in an almost straight line below mews cottages, as it heads towards Hyde Park. Several of the streets have clear references to the river beneath: Upbrook Mews and Brook Mews North. The mews were built within the valley of the river so are much lower than the adjacent streets.

Right: Brook Mews North. Far right: Horses watering on the River Westbourne. Bottom right: The Italian Gardens, Hyde Park.

5 Bays watering hole

By the late-fourteenth century, an area close to the north of what is now Hyde Park had become known for the watering of horses (bays). A reservoir, fed by the River Westbourne, supplied drinking water for horses and riders alike on their way into or out of London. The thoroughfare later became known as Bayswater Road.

River Westbourne

Lancaster Gate Underground

Bayswater Rd

Gloucester Terrace

Craven Road

Brook Mews North

Upbrook Mews

Elm Mews

Gloucester Mews West

Craven Terrace

HYDE PARK

6 The Italian Gardens

Queen Caroline, wife of George II, had the river dammed in 1730 to create a new lake. The original ponds were created as filter beds in an attempt to clean the polluted Westbourne before it entered the Serpentine. However, the filter beds failed in their task, and by the 1850s it was decided to pipe the Westbourne around the lake. In 1860, on the instructions of Prince Albert, the Italian Gardens were created and designed by Sir James Pennethorne. The original filter beds became the ornamental ponds, with fountains being powered by a steam engine located within the building to the north of the ponds (now the pavilion, *right*). Water for the ponds and the Serpentine are now taken from a borehole.

Walking these pages: 2.5km

33

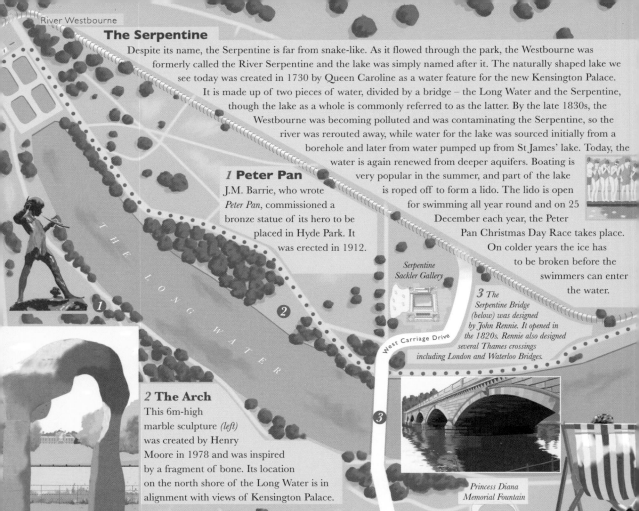

River Westbourne

The Serpentine

Despite its name, the Serpentine is far from snake-like. As it flowed through the park, the Westbourne was formerly called the River Serpentine and the lake was simply named after it. The naturally shaped lake we see today was created in 1730 by Queen Caroline as a water feature for the new Kensington Palace. It is made up of two pieces of water, divided by a bridge – the Long Water and the Serpentine, though the lake as a whole is commonly referred to as the latter. By the late 1830s, the Westbourne was becoming polluted and was contaminating the Serpentine, so the river was rerouted away, while water for the lake was sourced initially from a borehole and later from water pumped up from St James' lake. Today, the water is again renewed from deeper aquifers. Boating is very popular in the summer, and part of the lake is roped off to form a lido. The lido is open for swimming all year round and on 25 December each year, the Peter Pan Christmas Day Race takes place. On colder years the ice has to be broken before the swimmers can enter the water.

1 Peter Pan

J.M. Barrie, who wrote *Peter Pan*, commissioned a bronze statue of its hero to be placed in Hyde Park. It was erected in 1912.

THE LONG WATER

Serpentine Sackler Gallery

West Carriage Drive

3 The Serpentine Bridge *(below)* was designed by *John Rennie. It opened in the 1820s. Rennie also designed several Thames crossings including London and Waterloo Bridges.*

2 The Arch

This 6m-high marble sculpture *(left)* was created by Henry Moore in 1978 and was inspired by a fragment of bone. Its location on the north shore of the Long Water is in alignment with views of Kensington Palace.

Princess Diana Memorial Fountain

Hyde Park

The area now known as Hyde Park was once owned by the Abbot of Westminster Abbey and the river that flowed through it was partially dammed to created fishponds. During the Reformation, Henry VIII seized the land and raised the dam to create a small lake to attract deer and boar. The park became a royal hunting ground. In 1689, not long after Hyde Park was opened to the public, William II created Kensington Palace, a royal residence on the western flank of the park. In 1851, Hyde Park was used as the site for the Great Exhibition before its removal to Crystal Palace *(see page 76)*. Today, the land is a Royal Park of 142 hectares and is used by many Londoners and tourists alike for recreational activities, including walking, jogging, boating and swimming.

A SUPPLY OF WATER BY CONDUIT FROM THIS SPOT WAS GRANTED TO THE ABBEY OF WESTMINSTER WITH THE MANOR OF HYDE BY KING EDWARD THE CONFESSOR. THE MANOR WAS RESUMED BY THE CROWN IN 1536 BUT THE SPRINGS AS A HEAD AND ORIGINAL FOUNTAIN OF WATER WERE PRESERVED TO THE ABBEY BY THE CHARTER OF QUEEN ELIZABETH IN 1500.

River Westbourne

4 *The Tyburn Brook is a small tributary of the Westbourne and it rises close to the former site of execution near Marble Arch. It is not to be confused with the River Tyburn.*

5 *Left: A plaque with a brief history of local water supply.*

5

(alternative route)

The Holocaust Memorial

6

4

THE SERPENTINE

Rotten Row

Open-air concerts have become a major feature of the summer in Hyde Park, with bands such as Queen, the Rolling Stones, Pink Floyd and Blur playing live. Towards the north-east of the park is Speakers' Corner, which has become the location of protest and debate. Famous speakers have included Karl Marx, Vladimir Lenin, Ben Tillett and George Orwell.

The Lido

6 The Dam

The ornamental dam has an overflow that allows the surplus water from the lake to cascade down to form a short river which runs into the Ranelagh Sewer. While this is not actually the Westbourne flowing off the lake, it does follow the route the river once took.

Walking these pages: 1.8km

N

South Carriage Drive

Knightsbridge

1 The Knight's Bridge

The Knight's Bridge, which crossed the Westbourne to the south of Hyde Park, gave its name to the area. Until residential housing appeared in the late eighteenth century, travelling though this wooded area was fraught with risk of robbery and attack. The river at this time was still uncontaminated but was prone, due to the large watershed, to flash flooding.

Left: The stone Knight's Bridge over the Westbourne c.1400. Right: The Pantechnicon on Motcomb Street. Below: Water's Murmur, a steel relief showing the River Westbourne.

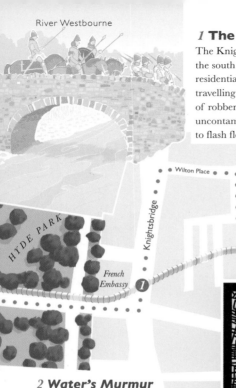

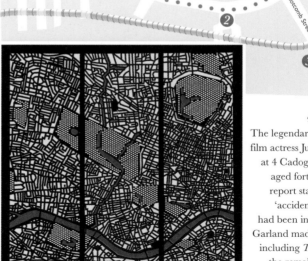

2 Water's Murmur

In the entrance to a new residential block is a 3m square steel relief depicting the route of the Westbourne from Paddington to the Thames *(right)*. Entitled *Water's Murmur*, it was created in 2009 by Julian Stocks and, aptly, was cut using a waterjet.

4 Judy Garland

The legendary American singer and film actress Judy Garland *(right)* died at 4 Cadogan Lane, in June 1969, aged forty-seven. The coroner's report stated that her death was 'accidental', though her health had been in decline for some time. Garland made over two dozen films including *The Wizard of Oz* and the remake of *A Star is Born*.

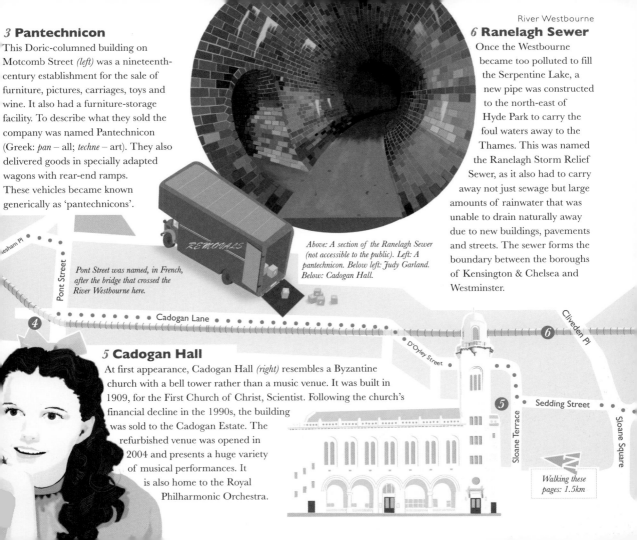

3 Pantechnicon

This Doric-columned building on Motcomb Street *(left)* was a nineteenth-century establishment for the sale of furniture, pictures, carriages, toys and wine. It also had a furniture-storage facility. To describe what they sold the company was named Pantechnicon (Greek: *pan* – all; *techne* – art). They also delivered goods in specially adapted wagons with rear-end ramps. These vehicles became known generically as 'pantechnicons'.

6 Ranelagh Sewer

River Westbourne

Once the Westbourne became too polluted to fill the Serpentine Lake, a new pipe was constructed to the north-east of Hyde Park to carry the foul waters away to the Thames. This was named the Ranelagh Storm Relief Sewer, as it also had to carry away not just sewage but large amounts of rainwater that was unable to drain naturally away due to new buildings, pavements and streets. The sewer forms the boundary between the boroughs of Kensington & Chelsea and Westminster.

Above: A section of the Ranelagh Sewer (not accessible to the public). Left: A pantechnicon. Below left: Judy Garland. Below: Cadogan Hall.

Pont Street was named, in French, after the bridge that crossed the River Westbourne here.

5 Cadogan Hall

At first appearance, Cadogan Hall *(right)* resembles a Byzantine church with a bell tower rather than a music venue. It was built in 1909, for the First Church of Christ, Scientist. Following the church's financial decline in the 1990s, the building was sold to the Cadogan Estate. The refurbished venue was opened in 2004 and presents a huge variety of musical performances. It is also home to the Royal Philharmonic Orchestra.

Walking these pages: 1.5km

1 Blandel Bridge

At 56 Sloane Square a sandstone plaque *(right)* marks the site of the Blandel Bridge, which once straddled the River Westbourne at this point. It was earlier known as the Bloody Bridge due to the number of attacks and robberies that took place here.

2 Westbourne over Underground

Stand on either platform of the Underground station at Sloane Square and you will see a large 3m pipe above head height. This iron conduit is carrying the River Westbourne (Ranelagh Sewer) southwards. When a bomb fell on the station during a German aerial raid in November 1940, seventy-nine people were killed but the pipe remained intact.

Above: Blandel Bridge plaque.
Below right: The Royal Chelsea Hospital.
Below left: The Westbourne conduit over the platform at Sloane Square Underground.

In the event of the Royal Chelsea Hospital grounds being closed, use the alternative route

3 Royal Chelsea Hospital

Up until the 1850s, the Westbourne flowed as an open stream through Knightsbridge and Chelsea. The stream was also a water feature running through the grounds of the Royal Chelsea Hospital and Ranelagh Gardens. The hospital was founded in 1682 by Charles II to house injured and retired soldiers. The grand three-sided Baroque structure was designed by Sir Christopher Wren around the central Figure Court with a splendid vista of the River Thames beyond. Several of the buildings are still home to retired soldiers. Known as Chelsea Pensioners, they are very visible in their bright scarlet uniforms. The grounds are home to the Chelsea Flower Show each year.

Sedding St

Sloane Square Underground

Sloane Square

Holbein Place

Pimlico Road

Royal Hospital Road

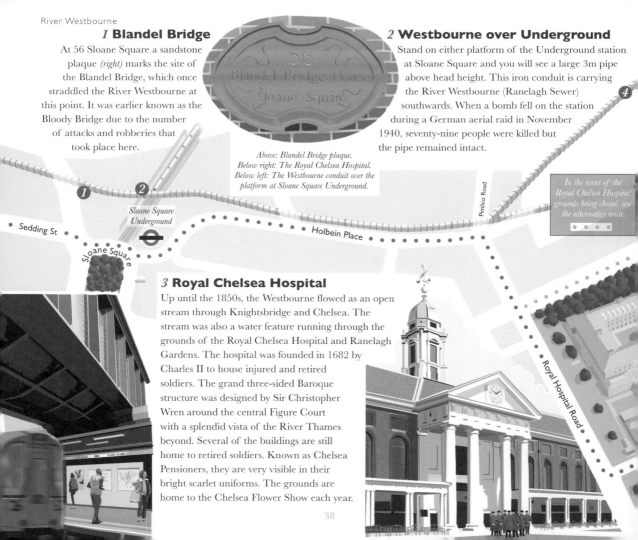

4 The Chelsea Waterworks

Until 1723, this spur of the River Westbourne flowed into the Thames just east of where Chelsea Bridge now stands. The Chelsea Waterworks Company intercepted the stream to supply parts of western London with water, once it had been filtered.

(alternative route)

Chelsea Bridge

Chelsea Bridge Road

RIVER THAMES

5 Mozart at the Pleasure Gardens

The Ranelagh Pleasure Gardens were founded in 1742 to provide, for those who could afford the entrance fee, entertainment in the form of music, dance and fireworks. Much of this was provided within the 45m wooden Rotunda. The garden was considered more upmarket than several of the other Pleasure Gardens around London at the time. In June 1764, an eight-year-old prodigy, Wolfgang Amadeus Mozart, played the harpsichord here at a charity concert.

Chelsea Embankment

6 The outfall

The Westbourne only flows into the Thames at times of heavy downpours, as most of the water is intercepted into the sewage system. The outfall gate can best be viewed from Chelsea Bridge at low water.

Left: Eastern wing of the Royal Chelsea Hospital. Above: Mozart at the Rotunda, Ranelagh Pleasure Gardens.

East Road

Right: The Westbourne outfall into the Thames at low tide.

Walking these pages: 1.2km

39

RIVER TYBURN

Complete walk 11.2km

The River Tyburn rises about 460m south of Hampstead Underground station and flows roughly in a south-south-eastward direction towards the Thames at Pimlico. A separate tributary rises further east on Haverstock Hill and joins the western arm in Swiss Cottage. The area around which the Tyburn rises was once a meadow west of Hampstead Heath.

The name Tyburn has evolved from the word *teo-burna*, meaning 'two streams', from which it grew. As it flowed through the parish of Marylebone, it once formed a border between two large estates. The name Marylebone has corrupted from 'St Mary's (church) by the Bourne (stream)'. Although the river is now completely subterranean, its path can still be detected on maps of the area, as several streets follow the original meandering line of the stream, breaking up the grid of the West End.

Arguably, the Tyburn could claim to have some royal appointment, as it flows immediately beneath Buckingham Palace. The Victorian journalist John Hollingshead wrote in 1862, after exploring the Tyburn from within the sewer pipe under the Palace, *'Of course my loyalty was at once excited, and, taking off my fan-tailed cap, I led the way with the National Anthem, insisting that my guides should join in the chorus'*.

Heath St · · · Fitzjohn's Avenue · · ·
Hampstead Underground

Left: A statue of Sigmund Freud by Oscar Nemon. Located on the corner of Fitzjohn's Avenue and Belsize Lane.

FOR THE·GOOD·OF THE·PUBLIC·THIS FOUNTAIN·IS·ERECTED NEAR·THE·SITE·OF AN·ANCIENT·CONDUIT KNOWN·AS·THE SHEPHERD'S WELL

1 Shepherd's Well

Unlike most of the other wells of Hampstead, this one dispenses pure water, untainted by minerals. The well, located on the corner of Fitzjohn's Avenue and Lyndhurst Road was, 200 years ago, surrounded by meadows and open fields. Though no longer visible, the well is the main source of the Tyburn. During the 1854 cholera outbreak, a wealthy woman of the area who was used to the waters from the Broad Street pump in Soho had it brought up in flasks. She died as a result, while all the local Shepherd's Well drinkers survived.

Shepherd's Path · *Lyndhurst Rd* · *Akenside Rd* · *Nutley Terrace* · *Daleham Gardens* · *Fitzjohn's Avenue*

Above left: A plaque marking the location of the Shepherd's Well.

2 Tavistock and Portman NHS Foundation Trust

The clinic is a specialist mental health facility that opened in 1920, in Tavistock Square, London. It initially offered psychological therapies for shell-shocked soldiers of the First World War. Following the Second World War, the clinic became part of the NHS, providing psychiatric training to medical students and a range of treatments including child and adolescent psychotherapies. It moved to this site *(right)* in 1967. There is a statue of the psychoanalyst Sigmund Freud *(left)* outside the building, on Fitzjohn's Avenue. He lived nearby in Maresfield Gardens until his death in 1939.

3 Palmer's Fountain

On the junction of College Crescent and Fitzjohn's Avenue sits an octagonal gothic granite drinking fountain *(left)*. The fountain, no longer in use, was erected in 1904 as a memorial to Samuel Palmer, who died the year earlier. Palmer, along with his brothers, were the owners of the Huntley & Palmer biscuit company in Reading. The house opposite the fountain on College Crescent, Palmers Lodge, became his London residence and is now a boutique hostel. Today, a flower stall is usually located in front of the fountain.

4 Royal Central School of Speech and Drama

This school was founded by Elsie Fogerty at the Royal Albert Hall in 1906. It moved to its current location, the former Embassy Theatre, in 1957 and offers students a huge range of theatrical skills from acting and speech craft to stage management and design. Some of its notable alumni, including Harold Pinter, Laurence Olivier and Peggy Ashcroft, have their names engraved on the steps of the school *(left)*. The school, as well as its royal prefix, has a physical connection with the monarchy, as the River Tyburn, which passes under the school, also passes under Buckingham Palace, some 6km to the south.

Above: The steps with names of famous former students who attended he Royal Central School of Speech and Drama.

Right: The eastern tributary of the Tyburn rises close to Haverstock Hill.

Left: The Swiss Cottage Library.

Walking these pages: 2.6km

5 Swiss Cottage Library

The library, with its striking vertical concrete slats, opened in 1964. The design, by Basil Spence, was to be part of a much larger civic centre for Swiss Cottage. However, due to local government reorganisation, the civic centre was never built.

River Tyburn

1 The Regent's Canal through the Park

In 1812, the architect and planner John Nash began promoting the idea of a canal that would link the Grand Junction Canal to the Thames at Limehouse. Previously, goods arriving at Paddington by barge had to be moved on to wagons and carried across London to the new docks in the East End. After numerous legal, engineering and financial problems the canal opened in 1820. The original plan for the canal was for it to cut across Regent's Park as a water feature, but the owners of the new adjacent houses objected to an industrial waterway spoiling their view. So instead the canal arched around the park in an embankment.

Regent's Park   Regent's Canal

River Tyburn

River Thames

4 Winfield House

Winfield House has been home to the United States ambassador since 1955. The neo-Georgian building was originally designed and built in 1937 for Barbara Hutton, the granddaughter of Frank Winfield Woolworth, heiress of the Woolworth store empire. After the war it was sold to the United States government for one dollar.

Macclesfield Bridge

Outer Circle

Avenue Road

Allitsen Road

Townsend Rd

Prince Albert Road

Mackinennal Street

Chalbert St

2 Chalbert Footbridge

The River Tyburn passes over the Regent's Canal in an aqueduct contained within the footbridge *(below)*.

3 The Terry Houses

Regent's Park is surrounded by numerous large stuccoed buildings, many designed by the park's creator, John Nash, in the early 1800s. The six houses that line the south bank of the canal, just west of Chalbert Bridge, were designed and built between 1988 and 2004 by the architects Quinlan & Francis Terry, as pastiches of seventeenth- and eighteenth-century European architectural styling.

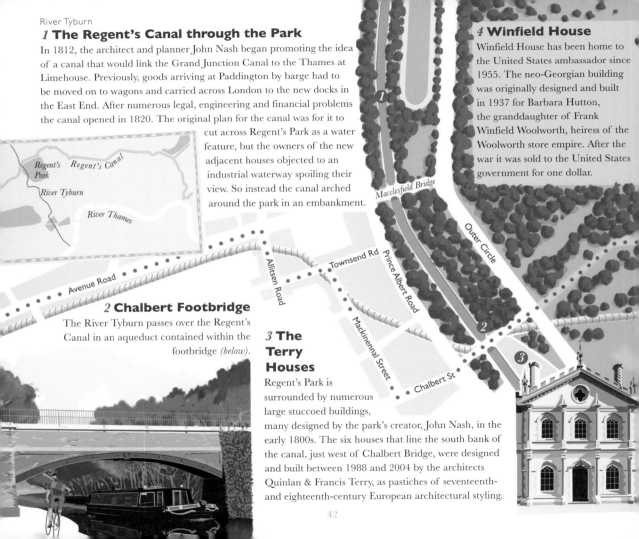

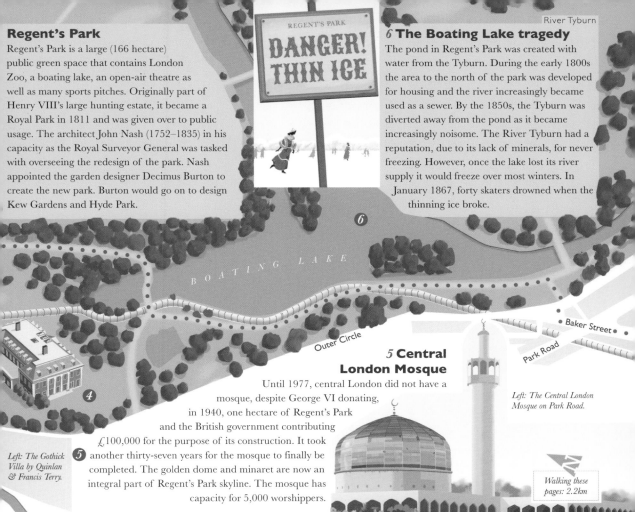

Regent's Park

Regent's Park is a large (166 hectare) public green space that contains London Zoo, a boating lake, an open-air theatre as well as many sports pitches. Originally part of Henry VIII's large hunting estate, it became a Royal Park in 1811 and was given over to public usage. The architect John Nash (1752–1835) in his capacity as the Royal Surveyor General was tasked with overseeing the redesign of the park. Nash appointed the garden designer Decimus Burton to create the new park. Burton would go on to design Kew Gardens and Hyde Park.

REGENT'S PARK

DANGER! THIN ICE

6 The Boating Lake tragedy

The pond in Regent's Park was created with water from the Tyburn. During the early 1800s the area to the north of the park was developed for housing and the river increasingly became used as a sewer. By the 1850s, the Tyburn was diverted away from the pond as it became increasingly noisome. The River Tyburn had a reputation, due to its lack of minerals, for never freezing. However, once the lake lost its river supply it would freeze over most winters. In January 1867, forty skaters drowned when the thinning ice broke.

BOATING LAKE

Outer Circle

Baker Street

Park Road

Left: The Central London Mosque on Park Road.

5 Central London Mosque

Until 1977, central London did not have a mosque, despite George VI donating, in 1940, one hectare of Regent's Park and the British government contributing £100,000 for the purpose of its construction. It took another thirty-seven years for the mosque to finally be completed. The golden dome and minaret are now an integral part of Regent's Park skyline. The mosque has capacity for 5,000 worshippers.

Left: The Gothick Villa by Quinlan & Francis Terry.

Walking these pages: 2.2km

43

River Tyburn

Baker Street
Underground

1 The Tyburn underground

Within Baker Street Underground station, at the western end of the Hammersmith & City and Circle line platforms, peer into the gloom of the tunnel *(right)* and you will see a large, dirty white structure traversing over the tracks. This is the River Tyburn. The line and station form part of the world's first underground railway that opened in January 1863. It originally ran between Paddington and Farringdon, with the carriages being hauled by steam engines. The Underground engineers, faced with the Tyburn cutting right across their planned line, had to carry the river over the tracks in a reinforced cast-iron pipe.

Above: An eastbound Circle line Underground train arrives at Baker Street station, passing under the River Tyburn aqueduct.

Baker Street

Blandford Street

Dorset Street

Gloucester Place

Melcombe Street

Glentworth St

Marylebone Road

Marylebone Lane

Wigmore Street

Oxford Street

2 Marylebone Lane

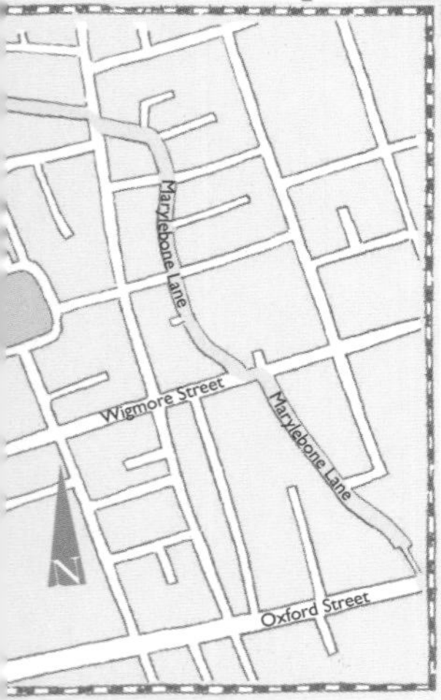

Marylebone Lane, shown in blue on the map *(left)*, breaks through the street grid of the West End. The street follows the course of the river.* Originally a country lane would have followed the river and this has been preserved within the town plan. Also builders would, if possible, avoid building over streams. * *Following a diversion it only flows along the upper half now.*

Below: Elm water pipes within a trench prior to burial.

Tyburn rebranded

Many thousands of public executions in London took place at Tyburn (now called Marble Arch), about 700m to the west of where the river intersects Oxford Street. It was then an area well outside the populated districts of London. The last hanging took place here in 1783 and around this time new housing, for the wealthy, was going up north of what was then Tyburn Road. In a bid to remove the connotations of death and hangings and to rebrand the area, Tyburn Road was renamed a continuation of Oxford Street, which already existed further east.

OXFORD STREET W1
(FORMERLY TYBURN ROAD)

CITY OF WESTMINSTER

3 Marylebone Lane grate

At the junction of Marylebone Lane and Bulstrode Street is a manhole cover in the middle of the road. Standing above the cover, whilst keeping an eye out for traffic, you may be able to see and hear the River Tyburn flowing below.

4 St Christopher's Place

The Tyburn flows beneath the paving stones of this very narrow pedestrianised alleyway. St Christopher's Place contains numerous fashionable shops and cafés and is an oasis away from the shopping mayhem of Oxford Street.

5 The Great Conduit

The River Tyburn supplied the City of London with fresh water from as early as the thirteenth century. The river used to flow 100m further to the east, continuing south along the southern end of Marylebone Lane to Tyburn Road (now Oxford Street), close to what is now Bond Street Underground station. In 1236, the rights to remove water from the Tyburn were granted and an outfall was created close to what is now Stratford Place. By using hollowed-out elm trunks as pipes, the water flowed nearly 4km into Cheapside within the City. The Great Conduit finally opened in 1245. An ornate lead cistern located at the eastern end of Cheapside supplied water freely to the populace. To celebrate the coronation of Henry VI in 1432, red wine replaced water here. The wooden conduit was destroyed in the Fire of London in 1666 and was not replaced.

Above: The Great Conduit leading to Cheapside in the City of London.

Walking these pages: 1.8km

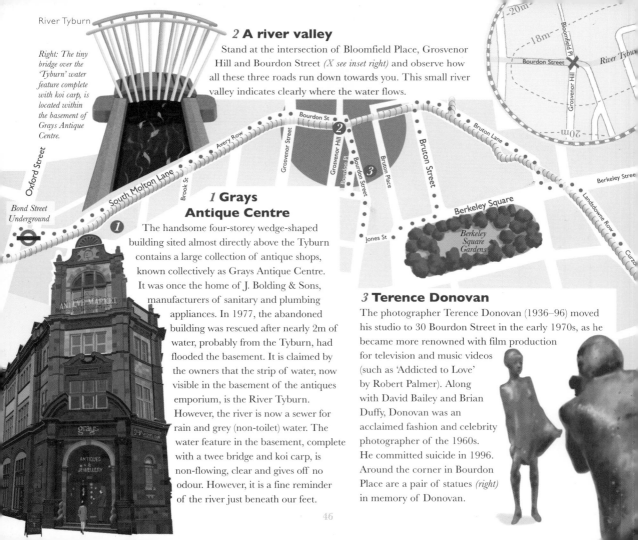

River Tyburn

Right: The tiny bridge over the 'Tyburn' water feature complete with koi carp, is located within the basement of Grays Antique Centre.

2 A river valley

Stand at the intersection of Bloomfield Place, Grosvenor Hill and Bourdon Street *(X see inset right)* and observe how all these three roads run down towards you. This small river valley indicates clearly where the water flows.

1 Grays Antique Centre

The handsome four-storey wedge-shaped building sited almost directly above the Tyburn contains a large collection of antique shops, known collectively as Grays Antique Centre. It was once the home of J. Bolding & Sons, manufacturers of sanitary and plumbing appliances. In 1977, the abandoned building was rescued after nearly 2m of water, probably from the Tyburn, had flooded the basement. It is claimed by the owners that the strip of water, now visible in the basement of the antiques emporium, is the River Tyburn. However, the river is now a sewer for rain and grey (non-toilet) water. The water feature in the basement, complete with a twee bridge and koi carp, is non-flowing, clear and gives off no odour. However, it is a fine reminder of the river just beneath our feet.

3 Terence Donovan

The photographer Terence Donovan (1936–96) moved his studio to 30 Bourdon Street in the early 1970s, as he became more renowned with film production for television and music videos (such as 'Addicted to Love' by Robert Palmer). Along with David Bailey and Brian Duffy, Donovan was an acclaimed fashion and celebrity photographer of the 1960s. He committed suicide in 1996. Around the corner in Bourdon Place are a pair of statues *(right)* in memory of Donovan.

4 Shepherd Market

The name of this area does not originate from sheep trading but more prosaically from the builder, Edward Shepherd, who developed the area in the 1740s, around Brook Field, through which the Tyburn ran. Shepherd Market was a part of Mayfair, which in turn took its name from the riotous carnival that occurred each year in the first half of May. The fair, was outlawed in the early eighteenth century, but the area maintained a reputation for bawdy and lewd entertainment. Until the late 1950s, Shepherd Market was notorious for 'street walkers'.

Right: The eastern façade of Buckingham Palace.

Green Park Underground

5 The Green Park

As you enter the Green Park from Piccadilly you will see how the park slopes away. To the right is a shallow river valley. The Tyburn was still visible here in 1837. However, the river's noxious smells and proximity to Buckingham Palace led to it being buried in a brick-lined conduit. In the eighteenth century a reservoir, fed by the Tyburn, was created within the park, for the Chelsea Waterworks Company to supply water to adjacent parts of the West End and Westminster. It was decommissioned shortly after the river went subterranean.

6 Buckingham Palace

Buckingham Palace is the London residence of the monarch of the United Kingdom and has been so since 1837. The palace, with its 775 rooms, was built in a haphazard fashion between 1700 and 1850 with principal architects being John Nash and Edward Blore. The Portland stone frontage we see today was not added until 1913. The Tyburn flows immediately below the front of the palace.

Walking these pages: 2.4km

Left: A sculpture of the model Twiggy and the photographer Terence Donovan by Neal French in Bourdon Place.

Thorney Island

The area to the south-east of Buckingham Palace was possibly once an island within marshland. The Tyburn, on its path to the Thames, split to form a delta *(see left)*. An early settlement founded the church of St Peter upon Thorney Island, a religious establishment that would eventually construct Westminster Abbey. Once Tyburn waters began being syphoned off to the City in the thirteenth century *(see page 45)*, the marshland may have started to dry out and the channels were covered over.

Left: The River Tyburn 'delta'.

King's Scholars' Pond Sewer

By the nineteenth century, the Tyburn, like so many other London rivers, had become extremely polluted and was really more of an open sewer than a river. Due to popular demand it was culverted in the 1830s and was renamed King's Scholars' Pond Sewer, as it took a water supply from the pond that sat within Vincent Square. The Square is now the playing fields of Westminster School, once the 'King's Scholars' school.

1 Westminster Cathedral

The Roman Catholic cathedral *(below)* is located on land that had once been the site of a prison, Tothill Fields Bridewell. The Tyburn bordered the prison's western flank. This was within an area that contained some of the worst slums in London. The cathedral was designed by the architect John Francis Bentley in a neo-Byzantine style of distinctive red brick and Portland stone stripes, complete with a single 87m-high slender campanile. It was felt at the time that a gothic design would have competed with the nearby ancient Westminster Abbey. The interior features over 100 types of marble but due to lack of funding it is, in places, still incomplete, with bare brick exposed. It was consecrated in 1910.

Left: A cross-section of the King's Scholars' Pond Sewer.

Victoria station & Underground

3 The Tyburn meets the Thames

The final 270m of the Tyburn was, until the late 1960s, an open storm drain. After the interceptor sewers had been installed in the 1860s, the river rarely reached the Thames except during heavy or prolonged rainfall, when the system could not cope and the water was redirected into the river. Late twentieth century pressure for more housing resulted in the final few hundred metres of the Tyburn being culverted. From Vauxhall Bridge or St George Wharf on the south shore, the Tyburn's entrance into the Thames is quite visible at low water as a large semi-circular tunnel. Above it sits a rebuilt version of Tyburn House. This used to be lodgings for the sewermen.

Thomas Cubitt's Pimlico

In 1824, Richard Grosvenor, 2nd Marquis of Westminster, commissioned Thomas Cubitt to create a vast new residential estate of squares and crescents upon his land in Pimlico and Belgravia, to house the growing middle class population of London. These areas had previously been occupied by market gardens. Modern building techniques were introduced by Cubitt to create the stuccoed residences in record time. The Tyburn was by now a stinking sewer flowing through Pimlico. Cubitt campaigned successfully to have it culverted.

Top: Tyburn House and the Tyburn's outfall into the Thames.
Above: A wall plaque by the Thames describing the route of the Tyburn.

Top: A stuccoed street in Pimlico. Right: A drain cover on the intersection of Tachbrook and Charlwood Streets.

2 The Tyburn below

At the crossroads of Tachbrook and Charlwood Streets, peer into the metal drain cover, whilst keeping a very careful eye out for traffic. Here you should hear (and possibly see) the Tyburn flowing some 5m below.

Walking these pages: 2.2km

Pimlico Underground

RIVER FLEET

Complete walk from Vale of Health 9.3km
Complete walk from Kenwood House 10.8km (page 52)

The Fleet, arguably London's most famous hidden river, rises in two locations on Hampstead Heath, unites in Camden and flows south-eastwards into the Thames under Blackfriars Bridge. Over the past 2,000 years the river has been given numerous names: Fleot, River of Wells, Fleet Ditch and by the Thames: the New Canal.

In 1832, the river was referred to as *'the silvery Fleet [that] still meanders, irrigating those charming meadows which reach on either side of Kentish Town.'** Around King's Cross there were numerous wells that fed into the river and by what is now Farringdon station were the gardens belonging to the Bishop of Ely, which led steeply down to the banks of the river. However, by the mid-nineteenth century the Fleet had succumbed to the forces of Mammon. Economic pressures from a burgeoning capital had forced the river underground.

The Fleet has been associated with both good health and disease in equal measures. Many wells were located along the course of the river with mineral-rich waters that many people believed had therapeutic values. The ponds on the Heath, which are still in use today for recreational purposes, were created to supply parts of London with clean water.

As more and more industries sprang up, the river became used as a dumping ground for refuse and detritus. Mills, tanneries and a meat market would dispose of unwanted produce straight into the Fleet. The river and its immediate environs were no longer pleasant places to linger or reside. Fresh drinking water had to come from other sources and the 'silvery Fleet' had become a silted-up ditch.

The piecemeal process of culverting the river started in 1733. Only on Hampstead Heath can the waterway still be seen today.

*Anthony Crosby, introduction to Views of the Fleet.

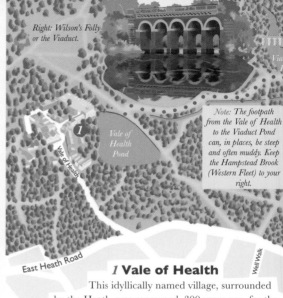

Right: Wilson's Folly or the Viaduct.

Note: The footpath from the Vale of Health to the Viaduct Pond can, in places, be steep and often muddy. Keep the Hampstead Brook (Western Fleet) to your right.

Vale of Health Pond

Vale of Health

East Heath Road

Well Walk

1 Vale of Health

This idyllically named village, surrounded by the Heath, was renowned, 300 years ago, for the unsavoury production of leather and varnish. It was, until the late eighteenth century, known as Hatchett's Bottom and stood adjacent to an unhealthy piece of bogland. The area was drained by the Hampstead Water Company to reduce the risk of waterborne diseases and create a new clean water supply to eighteenth-century London. It is also the source of the River Fleet on the western Heath. By 1800, the area had been rebranded as the Vale of Health. The author and poet D.H.Lawrence lived here in 1915.

Heath Street

Hampstead Underground

2 Mixed Bathing Pond

Though it is the smallest of all the swimming ponds on Hampstead Heath, it was the earliest officially designated bathing area of the three. During the late nineteenth century, more Londoners were learning to swim, rather than merely bathe. The Mixed Pond became very popular, as it was very close to the Hampstead Heath railway station and was also free, unlike the new Victorian pools. Today, it is very much an established part of the Hampstead Heath culture.

Sir Thomas Maryon Wilson

Hampstead Heath today, to the north and west, is largely populated with trees. This is not a typical 'heath' of gorse and scrub. However, 200 years ago, there were very few trees on the Heath, as can be seen in paintings by John Constable. In 1829, the Lord of the Manor, Sir Thomas Maryon Wilson, requested permission to build twenty-eight villas on his land. The viaduct *(far left)* was constructed as a planned road into the estate. His repeated applications were turned down. In an act of 'vandalism', he planted trees over much of his Heath and also created a brickworks south of the viaduct to exploit the resources of clay under his estate.

Taking the waters

In the early eighteenth century, Hampstead had become a fashionable spa resort, far removed from the squalor of London. Visitors to the Assembly and Pump Rooms on Well Walk would drink the mineral- and iron-rich chalybeate waters while being entertained with music and dance. It was widely believed at the time that these mineral waters had numerous medicinal qualities. The waters were also bottled *(left)* and sold in parts of London. The hard and soft waters of Hampstead Heath were useful for the washing and starching of clothes. From Tudor times, dirty linen was sent up to the washerwomen of Hampstead. Often wet clothing would be dried on the gorse bushes of the Heath.

Mixed Bathing Pond

No 2 Pond

No 1 Pond

East Heath Road

VALE OF HEALTH

Beware sudden drop

No Swimming

No Diving

In Emergency phone
Dial 999 hours
020 8340 5260

Hampstead Heath Overground

Agincourt Road

Mansfield Rd

River Fl

Southampton Rd

Walking these pages: 2.2km

Pond St

Fleet Road

River Fleet

1 **The Sham Bridge**

This 'bridge', visible at the eastern end of the
Thousand Pound Pond, is actually a façade
constructed in the late eighteenth century
by the owners of
Kenwood House.

*Kenwood House: best known
for its rear aspect overlooking
the Heath.*

Hampstead Lane

A cross section of upper
Hampstead Heath

Bagshot Sand

Claygate Beds

London Clay

2 **Kenwood House**

The word Ken, of Ken-wood, is derived from the old English word *caen*, meaning
'oak'. In 1764, the 1st Earl of Mansfield commissioned the neoclassical designer
Robert Adam to improve the house and grounds. Thirty years later, Humphry Repton
was appointed to redesign the estate and create a much grander feel. In 1927, the
house and grounds were acquired by the Earl of Iveagh and donated to the public.
The art collection includes work by Vermeer and Rembrandt, and the house is free
to enter. At the beginning of the nineteenth century, the view south from Kenwood
House would have included St Paul's Cathedral. Today, the trees obscure this view.

Stock
Pond

Millfield Lane

Thousand
Pound Pond

Wood Pond

Ladies'
Bathing
Pond

Bird
Sanct

Geology of the Heath

The northern and highest section of
Hampstead Heath is a layer of Bagshot
Sand, deposited 40 million years ago.
Beneath this sand is a 120m layer of
Claygate Beds and London Clay *(see above)*.
Rain falling on the sand filters through it
until it reaches the impervious clay, travels
horizontally and springs out as streams.
To the south of Kenwood House several
small rivulets can be seen, especially after
a heavy downfall. Four rivers flow out
from the Heath: the Fleet, the Tyburn, the
Westbourne and the Brent.

Hampstead Heath

The Heath is probably north London's most prized piece of open
land, covering 320 hectares. Two hundred years ago it was very
different. Several wealthy owners controlled much of the land.
Pressure from a burgeoning capital made the land more attractive
to housing development *(see Sir Thomas Maryon Wilson, previous page)*.
The Metropolitan Board of Works was given control of sections of the Heath in 1871
and it became common land. However, there were other pockets of land in private
ownership and at risk of development. Led by Robert Hunter and Octavia Hill, who
would later found the National Trust, they began to acquire
these estates and ease them over into public ownership. The
Heath is now managed by the City of London Corporation.

Spaniards Road

3 The Highgate Ponds

The ponds on the eastern side of the Heath are known as the Highgate Ponds. Two of the ponds are reserved for single-sex swimming. During the late seventeenth century, attempts were made to channel fresh water into the City from higher ground by creating reservoirs from the waters flowing off the Heath. The ponds also became makeshift bathing pools. Men would immerse themselves in the water to bathe but not to swim. Swimming was rarely practised or taught until later in the nineteenth century. Today, the swimming ponds are extremely popular, with some still believing in the healing qualities of the waters.

The Hampstead Water Company

Despite appearances, nearly all the ponds on the Heath are man-made. Parliamentary legislation in 1544 allowed for the channelling of water into London, though it was not until the late seventeenth century that the Highgate Ponds were created. The Hampstead Water Company dammed up the Highgate Brook to form seven reservoirs to supply water, at a price, to the population of Kentish Town, Camden and the City. The water was piped into London using hollowed-out elm trees. The 1852 Water Act brought an end to the practice of supplying water from the ponds, as it now had to be treated first. The Hampstead Water Company could not fulfil these obligations and sold its interests to the New River Company. The Fleet waters were used, for a while, as non-potable water for steam engines at St Pancras and soon after became a sewer.

River Fleet

4 Dartmouth Park

This area of housing was built during the late Victorian era for the professional classes. The Fleet, which flows along York Rise, was covered over before the houses were built and the steep sloping roads to the east indicate the valley along which the river flows.

3
Model Boating Pond

Millfield Lane

Highgate West Hill

Swain's Lane

Brookfield Park

4

Croftdown Road

York Rise

Men's Bathing Pond

Highgate No. 1 Pond

Walking these pages: 3.1km

River Fleet

Burghley Road

Lady Somerset Road

Burghley Road

Ⓘ

Junction Road

Kentish Town Underground & station

Highgate Road

Fortess Road

Holmes Road

Inkerman Rd

Cathcart St

1 Fleet over rail

At the end of York Rise, the road turns left into Churchill Road. Immediately to the right is a footbridge over the Gospel Oak to Barking railway line. On the bridge to the right is a large conduit *(above)* carrying the River Fleet southwards.

Below: Hampstead Heath with Lido and running track.

Ken Ditch Town

The eastern branch of the Fleet, flowing from Ken (or Caen) Wood, was often referred to as the Ken Ditch. It is very possible that the area Kentish Town takes its name from this.

Right: A bridge over the Fleet, Kentish Town, c.1800

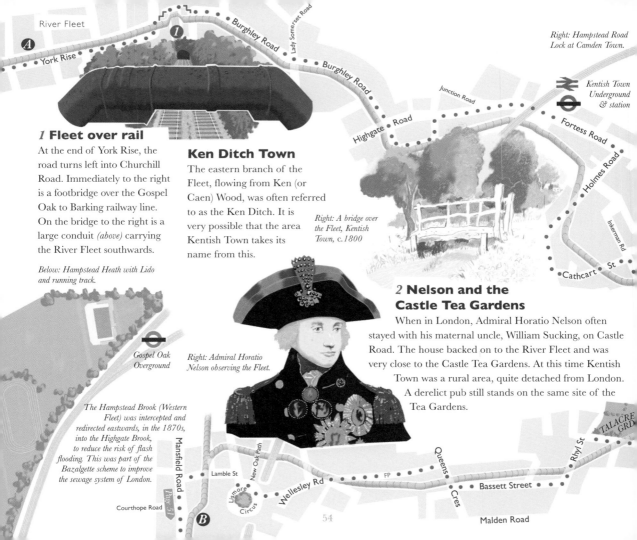

2 Nelson and the Castle Tea Gardens

When in London, Admiral Horatio Nelson often stayed with his maternal uncle, William Sucking, on Castle Road. The house backed on to the River Fleet and was very close to the Castle Tea Gardens. At this time Kentish Town was a rural area, quite detached from London. A derelict pub still stands on the same site of the Tea Gardens.

Gospel Oak Overground

Right: Admiral Horatio Nelson observing the Fleet.

The Hampstead Brook (Western Fleet) was intercepted and redirected eastwards, in the 1870s, into the Highgate Brook, to reduce the risk of flash flooding. This was part of the Bazalgette scheme to improve the sewage system of London.

Mansfield Road

TALACRE GRD

Rhyl St

Queens Cres

Bassett Street

Lamble St

New Oak Path

Lismore Circus

Wellesley Rd

FP

Page 51

Courthope Road

Ⓑ

Malden Road

4 The Regent's Canal

The Regent's Canal opened in 1820 and was created to link the Grand Union Canal spur, in Paddington, to the River Thames, at Limehouse, and the newly built West India Docks (now Canary Wharf). Raw materials and finished goods were shipped along this 'superhighway' for nearly 150 years. The canal was built over what was then referred to as the Fleet Ditch Sewer. By the turn of the nineteenth century, the Fleet was some 7m below street level. A newly created conduit carried it under the canal.

5 A Fleet grate

Just after a short cycle lane on Georgiana Street, opposite the Prince Albert pub, is a circular grate in the road. Keeping a sharp eye out for cars and bicycles, peer into the drain cover and you should, if it has rained recently, hear and possibly see the River Fleet below.

3 Rivers merge

The two branches of the Fleet merge at a point close to Quinn's pub on the corner of Kentish Town Road and Hawley Road.

6 Camden Market

Camden Market is a large sprawling complex of indoor and open-air market stalls. It is hugely popular with both locals and tourists. Open seven days a week, it can be extremely busy at weekends. The area is often referred to as Camden Lock, though no such lock exists. The buildings north of the Regent's Canal were established originally to service the canal industry with warehousing, a large horse stable and hospital. Following the decline of the canal as an industrial highway, the buildings, since 1975, have become a marketplace selling jewellery, art, clothing, bric-a-brac and fast food.

Camden Road Overground

Camden Town Underground

Prince Albert

Royal College Street

Angler's Lane

Prince of Wales Rd

Kelly St

Castle Rd

Lewis St

Castlehaven Road

les Rd

Kentish Town Road

Hawley Road

Clarence Way

Camden Road

Lyme Street

Georgiana Street

Camden Street

towpath

Regent's Canal

Railway bridge over Chalk Farm Road.

Harmood Street

Clarence Way

Wales Rd

CAMDEN LOCK

Walking these pages: A–C 3.5km B–C 2.9km

River Fleet

1 St Pancras Old Church

St Pancras was a young Roman citizen, who in AD 304 was beheaded for his Christian faith at the age of fourteen. It is claimed that St Pancras Old Church has been the site of Christian worship since seventh century and possibly earlier. The church, sited on raised land to the east of the River Fleet, fell into disrepair by the mid-nineteenth century. The structure was largely demolished and rebuilt complete with a new tower. By this time the Fleet had been covered over. The arrival of the adjacent St Pancras railway station in the 1860s required a reduction in size of the graveyard. The task of relocating many of the graves was managed by the young architect and author Thomas Hardy. Notable persons buried in the churchyard include Sir John Soane and the writer and promoter of women's rights Mary Wollstonecraft.

Below: St Pancras Old Church, by the uncovered Fleet, in 1815. The church was largely rebuilt some forty years later.

3 The Great Northern Hotel

The hotel *(right)*, designed by Lewis Cubitt (younger brother of Thomas Cubitt), opened in 1854 to serve the new railway station at King's Cross. The Italianate-styled curved façade of the building reflects the curve of the River Fleet. No architect then wanted to build a structure over a river, even if it was culverted. The hotel has recently been restored to its former glory.

The route follows Pancras Road, under St Pancras station.

St Pancras International station

Royal College Street

St Pancras Way

Pancras Road

Pancras Road

2 St Pancras International station

Designed in a Victorian Gothic Revival style by George Gilbert Scott, the railway station opened in 1868. Trains ran primarily to and from the Midlands. The station, saved from demolition in the 1960s, is now the UK terminal for high-speed Eurostar trains to Paris and Brussels, and is probably one of the finest railway stations in the world.

4 King's Cross station

The engineers of King's Cross station had to tunnel the railway tracks under the Regent's Canal, just to the north, as locomotive engines of the time could not haul trains up a steep gradient to clear the waterway. The station, which opened in 1852, was designed by the architects George Turnbull and Lewis Cubitt. Trains from King's Cross head to and from the north-east and Scotland.

Товарищ, жареную картошку будете?

6 Lenin's fish & chips

Vladimir Ilyich Ulyanov, better known as Lenin *(left)*, spent much of his time between 1902 and 1911 in London. Whilst living in King's Cross in 1905, Lenin, a Bolshevik revolutionary and first leader of the Russian Communist Party, developed a taste for the working-class meal of fish and chips. He and his wife frequented a fish and chip shop on King's Cross Road.

King's Cross station

Left: St Pancras station.
Far right: Handbill for St Chad's Garden.

King's Cross St Pancras Underground

King's Cross St Pancras Underground

Regent's Canal

York Way

Caledonian Road

Pentonville Road

King's Cross Road

St Chad's Place

Gray's Inn Road

Euston Road

St Chad's GARDEN
HEALTH RESTOR & PRESERVED

5 St Chad's Garden and Battle Bridge

St Chad's Garden was established by the river in the late eighteenth century. A feature of the popular pleasure gardens was the mineral spa, whose waters it was claimed had purgative powers. The development of the railway through the area and culverting of the Fleet closed the gardens. The area used to be known for a bridge that spanned the River Fleet at this point. Battle Bridge was believed to be the place where Boudica fought the Romans in AD 60, though this is now disputed. In 1830, a large statue to commemorate George IV was constructed in Battle Bridge and the area became known as King's Cross. Though the statue has long gone, the name remains.

*Comrade, fancy a chip?

Walking these pages: 2.0km

57

The River's revenge

In 1846, rancid gases from the Fleet accidentally ignited, causing great damage. A deluge of sewage was forced out of the sluice gate by the Thames and into many basements close to the conduit. The world's first underground railway was designed to run along the Fleet valley close to King's Cross Road. The river, although culverted by this time, had to be rerouted to make way for the railway. In 1862, during the engineering work the conduit carrying the Fleet ruptured and flooded the track with sewage, to a depth of 4m.

2 Mount Pleasant

This was formerly the site of the notorious Coldbath Fields Prison (Clerkenwell Gaol), where a spring of the same name fed into the Fleet. The prison closed in 1877 and the land was acquired by the General Post Office for a new sorting office. In a bid to rid itself of former associations, the area was renamed Mount Pleasant. The car park opposite the sorting office on Phoenix Place is one of the few Second World War bomb sites that has not been redeveloped.

Above: The culverted Fleet bursts free. Right: The Royal Mail sorting office.

Above: A stone plaque marking the entrance to the former Bagnigge Wells Spa on King's Cross Road.

1 Bagnigge Wells Spa

South of Camden, the river had many adjacent wells. These included the wells of St Pancras, St Chad's *(see previous page)*, Bagnigge, Clerk's *(see opposite page)*, Fagges and St Bride's. The area was referred to as the 'Land of Wells'. Bagnigge House, on King's Cross Road, is reputed to have been the country house of Nell Gwyn, actress and mistress to Charles II. In 1757, the owner of the house discovered a natural spring. The water contained chalybeate (iron) and had a reputation for its purgative effects. The Bagnigge Wells spa grew and, with its banqueting hall and grounds, it became a very popular mini pleasure gardens – a place for the affluent to 'take the waters' by the banks of the Fleet. As the growing city of the nineteenth century encroached upon the 'countryside' of Bagnigge Wells, the polluted Fleet was encased below ground. Bagnigge Wells' reputation as a spa began to decline and it finally closed in 1841.

Clerkenwell

Clerkenwell, just outside the north walls of medieval London, was beyond the jurisdiction of the City. Sited on the eastern bank of the Fleet, it became home and refuge for many groups whose opinions and actions were opposed to the monarchy or government of the time. After the Knights Templar were banished from the city, following their dissolution in the early fourteenth century, they established a new headquarters in Clerkenwell. Papists and Jesuits took refuge here to escape the Protestant rule of the Tudors, despite several being hanged on Clerkenwell Green. William Corbett spoke at a large meeting against the Corn Laws on the same spot in 1826. Lenin edited the Communist paper, *Iskra* (*The Spark*) in an office on the Green from 1902.

4 Set within Well Court, 'the Clerks' Well' is visible within a tiny dedicated museum. The well is named after the clerks of the parish.

5 The Rookeries

Despite its fragrant name, Saffron Hill became notorious by the mid-nineteenth century as a rookery: a warren of dilapidated and slum housing and a no-go area for outsiders. It was made infamous by Charles Dickens in his novel *Oliver Twist*. Fagin's lair was located within this area. The Fleet, to the east of Saffron Hill was described at the time as a '*black stream… dark and fetid*'.

Below: The river valley is so deep on Warner Street that a viaduct had to be built to carry Rosebery Avenue over it.

3 The Fleet below

Immediately outside the Coach and Horses pub on Ray Street is an iron grate in the road. Checking for traffic first, stand over the grate and listen. You can usually hear and see the River Fleet flowing beneath your feet.

The Bishop's Garden

A perusal of many street names just west of Farringdon Road reveals horticultural references: Hatton Garden, Herbal Hill, Saffron Hill and Vine Street. This area was once the gardens of the Bishop of Ely's London residence. The terrain ran steeply down to the then-open River Fleet. In 1572, Elizabeth I gave these lands over to her Chancellor, Lord Hatton.

Walking these pages: 1.2km

River Fleet

1 Smithfield Market

For over 800 years there has been a livestock and meat market on this site. Its location, close to both the River Fleet and the City, was vital: providing water for cleaning the carcasses and a market for the finished produce. Until the seventeenth century, waste matter and gore from the animals was often dumped directly into the river, making it a fetid and often unnavigable waterway. By the mid-nineteenth century the cattle market was moved further north to Islington, while Smithfield continued as the centre of meat trading.

Left: The Central Meat Market, Smithfield, designed by Sir Horace Jones in 1867 (Jones would later design Tower Bridge).

3 Fleet Prison

On the lower reaches of the Fleet, several prisons were located adjacent to the river. The Fleet Prison, established in the twelfth century, was encircled by a 3m moat. This water was the source of numerous outbreaks of cholera among the inmates. This extremely forbidding place was destroyed during the Peasants' Revolt in 1381. Later, in 1780, a mob attempted to raze the prison to the ground during the Gordon Riots. The prison was finally closed and demolished in 1846.

Charterhouse Street

Cowcross St.

Farringdon Road

Holborn Viaduct

Greville St.

Saffron Hill

2 Holborn Viaduct

As it approaches the Thames, the Fleet valley is steep sided, almost ravine-like. Before 1869, anyone wanting to cross over Farringdon Road would have had to drop down to the Fleet and up the other side. The opening of the cast-iron viaduct *(right)* vastly improved the flow of traffic in and out of the City. The four statues on the viaduct celebrate science, fine art, commerce and agriculture.

5 The Black Friar pub

This unique public house *(right)* sits close to what was the eastern bank of the River Fleet and on land that was once the site of a Dominican monastery. The monks wore black cloaks, thus giving the name to the location and the pub. The Arts and Crafts-designed interior of the wedge-shaped building is lined with over fifty types of marble.

7 Blackfriars Bridge

The removal of the old London Bridge in 1831 increased the tidal flow of the Thames to such an extent that it eroded the piers of the original Blackfriars Bridge. Its replacement, designed by Joseph Cubitt, was opened by Queen Victoria, on the same day she opened Holborn Viaduct, in 1869.

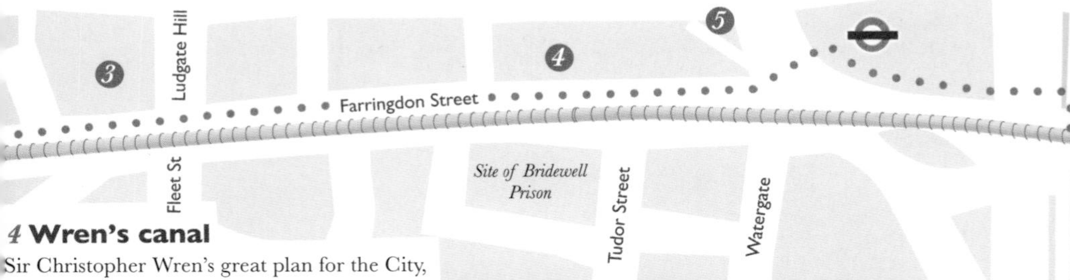

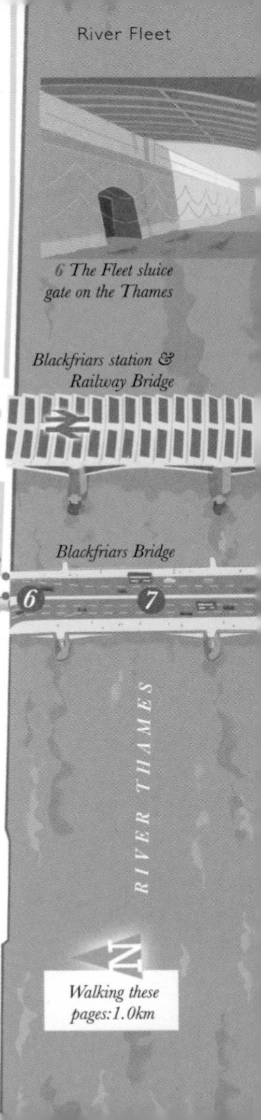

*Above:
Fleet Prison c.1800.*

River Fleet

6 The Fleet sluice gate on the Thames

Blackfriars station & Railway Bridge

Blackfriars Bridge

Ludgate Hill

Fleet St

Farringdon Street

Site of Bridewell Prison

Tudor Street

Watergate

Victoria Embankment

RIVER THAMES

Walking these pages: 1.0km

4 Wren's canal

Sir Christopher Wren's great plan for the City, following the Great Fire of 1666, included the canalisation of the Fleet: a Venetian vision of the Thames. The river was dredged of silt and rubbish and widened to allow larger ships to enter the new Fleet dockside, complete with purpose-built wharves *(right)*. However, the canal was not a commercial success and by the 1760s there was a greater need for a north–south road, so the Fleet canal was covered over as far as what is now Holborn Viaduct.

RIVER WALBROOK
Complete walk 2.8km

The Walbrook, running from north to south in between the two rises of Ludgate Hill and Cornhill, undoubtedly attracted the advancing Romans 2000 years ago; they built a fortress here by the side of the tidal Thames. The hills provided defensive strongholds while the Walbrook and its wells supplied fresh water and power for the mills. The small Walbrook estuary, now known as Dowgate, was an inlet suitable for several vessels to dock.

Clear streams rose at several locations close to what is now Shoreditch High Street, and several tributaries fed into the Walbrook; one, coming from Islington, followed the line of the City Road towards Old Street. There were several wells nearby too. One of these, Holywell, was renowned for its healing properties and a monastery was built on the site.

The river was a key source of power for milling and in the preparation of leather products and cutlery. However, it was also used as a place to discard detritus, effluent and dead animals. This once 'sweet smelling river' was, by the Middle Ages, a stinking sewer. By the late-sixteenth century, the Walbrook north of Dowgate had been entirely culverted and hidden from sight.

Prior to the twentieth century, old demolished buildings were rarely removed from the site. Some timber and stone may have been reused but the rubble was built over. The Walbrook valley was simply filled in, and as a result the river is now, in places, some 10m below street level.

How the Walbrook gained its name is not certain. The Saxon name for it was Gallobroc, which may have evolved into its current name or it was simply the brook that ran through the (Roman) wall.

Right: St Leonard's Church, Shoreditch.

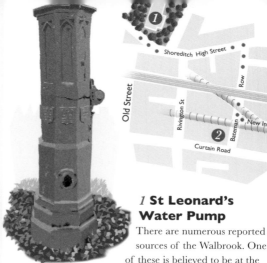

1 St Leonard's Water Pump

There are numerous reported sources of the Walbrook. One of these is believed to be at the water pump *(above)* by St Leonard's Church in Shoreditch. Though no long working, the vandalised pump once drew water up from the gravel strata below. The medieval church of St Leonard's was rebuilt in 1736 with a 58m steeple *(left)*. The church is referred to in the children's nursery rhyme 'Oranges and Lemons': '*When I grow rich, say the bells of Shoreditch.*'

2 The Holywell

Another source of the river was a 'holy' well within the grounds of the Priory of John the Baptist. It was claimed that the carbonated water from the well had healing properties. The priory was closed in the 1530s, on the orders of Henry VIII, along with many religious institutions loyal to the Pope. The priory was left to fall into ruin. It is believed that the well was located close to Bateman Row.

Shoreditch High Street Overground

3 The Theatre

By the sixteenth century, theatres and other entertainments were not permitted within the City of London, but could be established outside its walls.

In 1576 a playhouse, simply called the Theatre _(left)_ was constructed within the grounds of the former priory. Players at the Theatre included William Shakespeare's company, the Chamberlain's Men. The entrance was on Curtain Road alongside of which ran the Walbrook. In 1598, the Theatre, following a dispute with the landowner, was dismantled and moved, piece by piece, to Southwark.

5 Broadgate

Broadgate is a large office and retail estate that covers 13 hectares _(right)_. It was built over the site of the former Broadgate railway station and the River Walbrook. It is largely a pedestrianised area and during the winter months an open-air ice rink is installed within the complex.

River Walbrook

4 Worship St Drinking Fountain

At the right-hand end of a terrace row, a drinking fountain of marble and stone was installed in 1863, complete with a gothic arch and small alcove and door _(left)_. The fountain no longer works and almost certainly was not connected to the Walbrook. This was, after all, after Dr John Snow's discovery that connected polluted water supplies with cholera. The short terraced row, built as shops with industrial basements, was designed in the Arts and Crafts style by the architect Philip Webb, a colleague of William Morris.

Liverpool Street station

Moorfield Marshes

When the Romans built a fortified barricade around Londinium, the Walbrook had to be fed through the wall (now the London Wall), via an aqueduct. At times this would have restricted the amount of water entering the city and may have flooded the land to the north. It may also have been an intentional defensive ploy.

Walking these pages: 1.7km

1 Roman aqueduct

The Walbrook was channelled through the Roman wall via a narrow aqueduct *(left)*, approximately 55m long and 1m high. It is believed that the openings at each end were barred to prevent blockages. The remains of this aqueduct were discovered in the mid-nineteenth century some 4m below current street level. They are not visible to the public.

2 St Margaret Lothbury

This site has been a designated place of worship since 1185. The current church was designed by Sir Christopher Wren in 1683–92, following the destruction of the previous structure in the Great Fire of London in 1666. The plain square tower was added some eight years later. Built on the western side of the culverted Walbrook, it is believed that a small tributary of the river used to flow under the church. St Margaret Lothbury *(left)* now contains several original pieces of fine woodwork salvaged from other demolished Wren churches. It is still used as a parish church and is a Grade I listed building.

This page, clockwise from top left: Roman aqueduct; Tivoli Corner; Bank of England; St Margaret Lothbury.

3 Tivoli Corner

This feature, an open corner on the Bank of England, is modelled on the Temple of Vesta, a shrine to the goddess of fire, in Tivoli, Italy. It is sited very close to the Walbrook. The corner is illuminated by an open oculus skylight *(above)*.

4 Bank of England

The central bank of the United Kingdom was established in 1694. Today it is an independent body with responsibilities for setting monetary policy and for issuing bank notes. The original site of the bank was further south in the Ward of Walbrook. In 1788, Sir John Soane (1753–1837) was appointed as surveyor of the bank and during his forty-five-year tenure he rebuilt and expanded the site, making the bank more fireproof and secure by increasing the defensive fort-like walls and barracks. Much of Soane's work was demolished in the 1920s during the rebuild *(left)*, designed by the architect Sir Herbert Baker.

5 Grocers' Hall

This is the home of the Worshipful Company of Grocers, formerly the Guild of Pepperers. Their role was to ensure the purity of spices. Today, they are involved in charitable work.

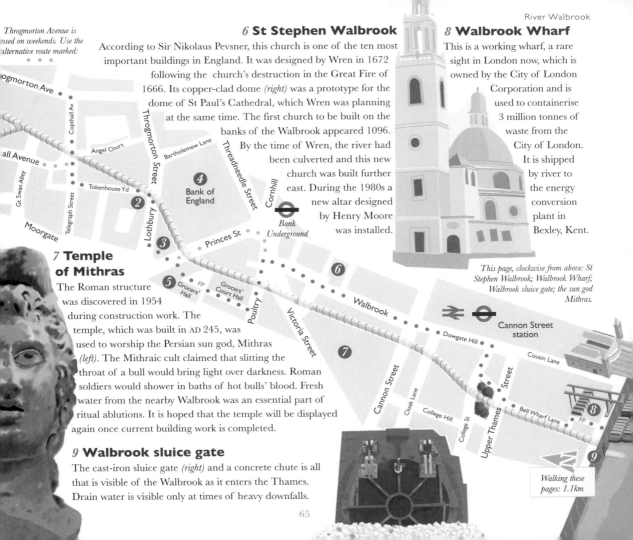

6 St Stephen Walbrook

According to Sir Nikolaus Pevsner, this church is one of the ten most important buildings in England. It was designed by Wren in 1672 following the church's destruction in the Great Fire of 1666. Its copper-clad dome *(right)* was a prototype for the dome of St Paul's Cathedral, which Wren was planning at the same time. The first church to be built on the banks of the Walbrook appeared 1096. By the time of Wren, the river had been culverted and this new church was built further east. During the 1980s a new altar designed by Henry Moore was installed.

8 Walbrook Wharf

This is a working wharf, a rare sight in London now, which is owned by the City of London Corporation and is used to containerise 3 million tonnes of waste from the City of London. It is shipped by river to the energy conversion plant in Bexley, Kent.

This page, clockwise from above: St Stephen Walbrook; Walbrook Wharf; Walbrook sluice gate; the sun god Mithras.

7 Temple of Mithras

The Roman structure was discovered in 1954 during construction work. The temple, which was built in AD 245, was used to worship the Persian sun god, Mithras *(left)*. The Mithraic cult claimed that slitting the throat of a bull would bring light over darkness. Roman soldiers would shower in baths of hot bulls' blood. Fresh water from the nearby Walbrook was an essential part of ritual ablutions. It is hoped that the temple will be displayed again once current building work is completed.

9 Walbrook sluice gate

The cast-iron sluice gate *(right)* and a concrete chute is all that is visible of the Walbrook as it enters the Thames. Drain water is visible only at times of heavy downfalls.

Throgmorton Avenue is closed on weekends. Use the alternative route marked:

Throgmorton Ave
Copthall Av
Angel Court
Bartholomew Lane
Throgmorton Street
Threadneedle Street
Cornhill
all Avenue
Gt Swan Alley
Tokenhouse Yd
Telegraph Street
Moorgate
Lothbury
Bank of England
Princes St
Bank Underground
Grocers' Hall
Grocers' Court Hall
Poultry
Victoria Street
Walbrook
Dowgate Hill
Cannon Street station
Cousin Lane
Cannon Street
Cloak Lane
College Hill
College St
Upper Thames Street
Bell Wharf Lane
Street
FP
FP

Walking these pages: 1.1km

HACKNEY BROOK

Complete walk 13km

Hackney Brook rises on the lower slopes of Hampstead Heath at two locations east and west of Holloway Road. They unite just north of the Emirates Stadium before heading east and then south-eastwards. Unlike all the other rivers featured in this guide, Hackney Brook does not flow directly into the Thames, but descends into the River Lee Navigation at Hackney Wick.

In the fifth century, a Danish lord named Haca (or Hacon) established a stronghold on an area of raised land or island (an 'eyot') above the marshes. The location became known as Hackney and the brook flowing through it took its name.

Daniel Defoe, while living in nearby Stoke Newington close to the brook, referred to Hackney in his *Tour Through the Whole Island of Great Britain* (1724–7) as being '…*so remarkable for the retreat of wealthy citizens, that there is at this time near a hundred coaches kept in it*'. At that time the village was still remote from London and considered a country retreat by those who could afford it.

By the mid-nineteenth century the brook had become so polluted and a danger to health that it was covered over. A much larger purpose-built sewer pipe replaced it. Known grandly as the Northern High Level Sewer, it follows the path of the brook from Holloway to Hackney Wick.

Above: The 45 rpm single 'Telstar' written and produced by Joe Meek. Below right: Joe Meek. Below left: The Odeon, Holloway Road.

2 Joe Meek

Joe Meek (1929–67) was a pioneering experimental record producer and songwriter in the early 1960s. Disillusioned with the established system of recording and producing pop records, he built his own studio in his flat at 304 Holloway Road. With musicians playing in various rooms of the apartment and Meek recording and manipulating the sounds in the kitchen, he created many hits, including 'Johnny Remember Me' by John Leyton and 'Telstar' by The Tornados. The latter went to number one in the pop charts. In 1967 he killed his landlady with a shotgun before turning it upon himself.

1 Odeon Holloway

Probably the most notable building on Holloway Road is the Odeon cinema. It was designed by C. Howard Crane (architect of the Earls Court Exhibition Centre – *see page 23*) and was opened in 1938 as the Gaumont. It was damaged by a doodlebug during the Second World War but was later restored and is now a Grade II listed building.

4 Gillespie Park

Gillespie Park is a 2.8-hectare nature reserve created out of railway marshalling yards, comprising grassland, woodland and ponds. It opened in 1983 as a green retreat for the local community and as an educational resource for schools.

5 The New River

The New River is a canal that was dug in 1613 to supply fresh water from springs in Hertfordshire into a reservoir at Sadlers Wells, Islington. Once it passed the reservoirs on Green Lanes it used to head south in a culvert. Originally the New River was carried over Hackney Brook in an embankment built of brick and timber. Though the New River still supplies water to Londoners, it no longer reaches Islington.

3 Arsenal FC

Arsenal Football Club moved into the Emirates stadium, on the site of the Ashburton Grove recycling plant, at the start of the 2006 season. Designed by Populous, who were also responsible for Wembley stadium, the ground seats 60,000 for Arsenal home games and the occasional Brazil international fixture. Statues and murals honouring Arsenal legends of the past surround the Emirates. The Art Deco east and west stands of 'Highbury', the stadium which served as home to Arsenal for ninety-three years, have been preserved and are located near the Arsenal Piccadilly line station.

Above and below: The Emirates Stadium. Right: Gillespie Park. Below right: The former Stoke Newington Pumping Station.

Hackney Brook

West Reservoir

Lordship Lane

Green Lanes

King's Cr

Queen's Drive

Blackstock Road

Mountgrove Road

Gillespie Road

4
GILLESPIE PARK

Arsenal Underground

Lowman Rd

Annette Rd

Hornsey Rd

Jackson Rd

Drayton Park

3

6 Stoke Newington Pumping Station

The 1852 Metropolis Water Act prohibited taking drinking water from the Thames. The New River Company at its Stoke Newington reservoir needed to increase its output and quality. So in 1856 six steam engines were installed, along with a water tower. The pump room housing, instigated by William Chadwell Mylne, resembled a Scottish baronial castle. By 1946 diesel pumps had replaced the steam engines and the building was surplus to requirement. It is now Grade II listed and functions as an indoor climbing centre.

N

Walking these pages: 4.9km

Hackney Brook

Manor Road

Bouverie Rd

Lordship Rd

Grayling Rd

Grazebrook Rd

Green Lanes

Stamford Hill

 Stoke Newington Overground

(Northwold Rd)

Maury Road

ABNEY PARK CEMETERY

2

CLISSOLD PARK

1

Left: Memorial stones in Abney Park Cemetery. Bottom left: Clissold House. Below: Hackney Downs.

Isaac Watts, a nonconformist theologian and hymn writer, lived in the Abney Hall before it became the cemetery. He often walked down to Hackney Brook for inspiration.

1 Clissold Park

The park was once formerly private land with an elegant neoclassical villa built around 1790. Within a century, the estate had been acquired by the Metropolitan Board of Works and was opened to the public. The New River used to flow past the house, though it is now an ornamental lake, and the two ponds to the north were once part of Hackney Brook. However, by the mid-nineteenth century, once the stream had become too polluted, it was diverted away. The two ponds were renamed after the men, Beck and Runtz, who campaigned to make the park a public open space. The villa, Clissold House, now serves as a café.

2 Abney Park Cemetery

The 12.5-hectare cemetery opened in 1840 following the need for more burial spaces beyond central London. Abney Park is a non-denominational place of rest (the first in Europe) with grounds that were never consecrated and is one of London's 'Magnificent Seven' cemeteries *(see page 20)*. With over 2,500 trees and shrubs, it is known as a garden cemetery, with the culverted Hackney Brook forming the northern border. The cemetery became bankrupt in 1972 and is now run by the Abney Park Trust. The grounds are overgrown but are very atmospheric, with thickets of ivy encasing many of the tombstones. Due to lack of space, there are only around five burials a year. Founders of the Salvation Army and nonconformists William and Catherine Booth are buried here.

3 Hackney Downs

This large 16-hectare area of open space includes football pitches, tennis courts and a bowling green. It was formerly common land but became a recreational ground in 1884. The downs have a very distinct decline towards the west. At the bottom of the valley runs Hackney Brook, though the stream is now buried beneath the raised railway line.

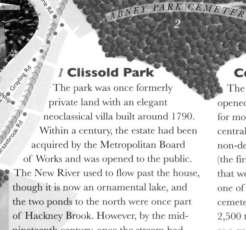

Right: St Augustine's tower. Far right: Sutton House. Below right: The Hackney Empire. Bottom right: Former watercress beds.

4 St Augustine's Tower

The distinct Grade I listed clock tower, standing at the top of Mare Street, was once part of St Augustine's medieval church (established in 1275) that stood by the banks of the Hackney Brook. By the late eighteenth century the church's capacity had been exceeded and plans were submitted to build a new larger church, St John's, nearby. In 1798 St Augustine's Church was demolished leaving only the tower. The tower is featured on the Borough of Hackney's coat of arms.

7 Sutton House

This early example of a brick-built house was commissioned in 1535 for Ralph Sadler, the right-hand man of Thomas Cromwell, chief minister to Henry VIII. The location of the house at the time was very rural and remote from the City and Westminster. Despite access to Hackney Brook within the gardens,

the household took its water from an adjacent well. Over the centuries, the house has been added to and amended, though it still retains much of its original medieval features and is the oldest residential building in Hackney. It is now owned and run by the National Trust.

HACKNEY DOWNS

5 The Hackney Empire

The 'Empire', is an ornate Edwardian music hall, designed by Frank Matcham and opened in 1901, with Charlie Chaplin, Stan Laurel and Marie Lloyd among the many who appeared here. From the 1950s until 1984, it served as a TV venue and later a bingo hall before being closed and threatened with demolition. Following a successful campaign to save the theatre, it reopened in 2004. The venue now hosts comedy, theatre, pantomime and opera events throughout the year.

Hackney Downs Overground

6 Until 1875, a watercress farm (right) was located where the Tesco supermarket is now. Until it was culverted, the farm drew water from the brook.

Hackney Central Overground

Walking these pages: 5.1km

1 Berger Paint Factory

In 1780 Lewis Berger, a German immigrant, established a paint factory on Morning Lane, adjacent to Hackney Brook (it was then aptly named Water Lane). Water for production was taken from a local well, noted for its purity. However, the brook was used to dispose of toxic waste products, until it was culverted 100 years later. Following several takeovers and mergers, the Homerton factory closed in 1960 and production was moved to Essex. Nothing of the site remains today though a local street and junior school carry the name Berger. Berger paints are now produced in India.

Homerton Overground

3 Victoria Park

Victoria Park was created in the 1840s as a parkland primarily for the working classes of the East End of London. The area was undergoing a massive industrial and residential expansion and public open space was desperately needed. The 86-hectare park was laid out by Sir James Pennethorne on land that was bounded on two sides by canals. The original plans included a lake and an arcaded shelter. Pennethorne would later go on to design Battersea Park. During the Second World War anti-aircraft guns were installed in the park to defend the East End against German bombers. This resulted in the park becoming a target in itself. The park is now the site of large music festivals in the summer. The first Rock Against Racism concert was held here in 1978.

Above left: The former Berger paint factory, Homerton. Below right: Top Lock on the Hertford Union Canal. Bottom right: The Burdett-Coutts drinking fountain (no longer functioning) within Victoria Park.

2 *The location of a silk mill upon the Hackney Brook. In the eighteenth century it employed up to 700 people.*

A12 East Cross Route

Cadogan Terrace

Kenworthy Road

Wick Road

Victoria Park Road

Wick Road

Morning Lane

4 River Lee Navigation

The Lee Navigation is a canalised section of the River Lea that runs down to the Thames. The warren of waterways that surrounds the Queen Elizabeth Olympic Park was originally created by medieval monks to drain the marshes and to channel streams into watermills for grinding flour. The Hackney Brook which flows into the Lee Navigation at Hackney Wick could be as wide as 30m at full flood.

Queen Elizabeth Olympic Park

Prior to the Olympic and Paralympic Games being held here in 2012, the land between the man-made complex of Bow Back Rivers and the Lee Navigation contained a few noxious works such as bone and chemical factories. However, much of the space was still marshland with allotments and wildlife in evidence. All of this was bulldozed away with the arrival of the Olympic Games. The newly landscaped Queen Elizabeth Olympic Park includes the Velodrome, the ArcelorMittal Orbit (the largest piece of art in the UK) and the London Aquatics Centre, designed by Zaha Hadid. The athletics stadium has been repurposed following the Games into a new football ground for West Ham United and is now named the London Stadium. Hackney Brook now links this football venue to the Emirates Stadium, Arsenal's ground. Both were designed by the same company, Populous.

Hackney Wick Overground

Above: The River Lee Navigation with the former Olympic stadium in the background. Below right: The Northern High Level Sewer crossing the River Lee Navigation.

Above: The London Stadium

5 Hertford Union Canal

The Hertford Union Canal was devised by Sir George Duckett, to link the Lee Navigation to the Regent's Canal and thus avoid the tidal River Thames. It opened for business in 1831. Unfortunately the fees charged to use the canal were prohibitive and the venture went bankrupt within a year. It was later bought out by the Regent's Canal Company.

6 The Greenway

The Northern High Level Sewer was built in 1861 as part of Bazalgette's grand plan to clean up a cholera-ridden capital *(see page 102)*. It follows the same valley that the Hackney Brook takes from Holloway. The sewage pipe, still in use today, continues on to the Beckton processing plant. The Greenway is a foot and cycle path that has been built above the pipes. It runs from Wick Lane and heads eastwards for 7km to Beckton.

Walking these pages: 3.0km

FALCON BROOK
Complete walk 9.6km

Falcon Brook is a small culverted stream that rises at several points on Streatham Hill. In its previous unculverted state it was hardly navigable, except for the last few hundred metres before it joined the Thames. For much of its length, the tributaries were historically referred to as the Hydeburn and the Woodbourne. However, by the seventeenth century, Sir Oliver St John, the new Lord of the Battersea manor, had renamed it Falcon Brook, after the rising falcon that appeared on the family crest.

Much of the land along the route of Falcon Brook was given over to market gardening. The area became famous for the asparagus and lavender that it sent to London. Numerous ponds and reservoirs for watering the plants were created upon the impervious clay, these being fed by the brook.

Following the arrival of the railways in the 1860s and the huge population expansion of London, mile upon mile of late-Victorian terraced rows were constructed over the market gardens. Though not as polluted as some of its neighbours, Falcon Brook was buried as the land become too expensive to leave as a water feature.

1 Falcon Brook below

At the intersection of Valley Road and South Oak Road, where the thoroughfare reaches its lowest point, there is a manhole cover in the middle of the road. Checking for traffic first, stand over the grate and listen. You can usually hear Falcon Brook flowing beneath your feet as it rushes off the steep-sided bowl to the east of Valley Road.

Right: manhole cover on Valley Road. Below: a ceramic flask of Streatham Spa water. Below left: Dr Samuel Johnson.

2 Streatham Spa

The first medicinal spring in Streatham was discovered in 1659, about 900m south of this location, on Streatham Common. By the mid-eighteenth century it had become extremely popular with visitors eager to drink the magnesium sulphate waters for their purgative effects. The waters were also bottled and shipped to London for sale. The essayist, critic and poet Dr Samuel Johnson was a frequent visitor to the spa from 1766 until his death eighteen years later. The route he took across Tooting Common is celebrated today, with a road named after him. The spa closed in 1792, at around which time a second Streatham Spa opened on Valley Road. Though not as popular as the first spa, it continued to operate until the twentieth century. A dairy bottling plant and distribution centre was built on the site. Local milk deliveries included the bottled spa water until the 1950s.

Streatham Hill
station

Bec not Beck

Tooting Bec is not named after a local stream but after a French monastery. Bec Abbey in Normandy, was donated a tract of land in Tooting following the Norman invasion in 1066.

4 Falcon Brook tributaries

Falcon Brook is made up of several tributaries. The longest stream shown on this page (running east to west) was once known as the Woodbourne. The northernmost tributary, formerly the Hydeburn (or Hildaburna) also rises on Streatham Hill and runs north-westwards until it joins the Westbourne and becomes Falcon Brook. Today, the entire set of streams are generally referred to as Falcon Brook.

Left: Tooting Bec fishing lake.
Below left: Tooting Bec Lido.

Tooting Commons

The Tooting Commons comprise two open spaces: Tooting Bec Common and Tooting Graveney Common. They once were communal space for grazing cattle and for the collection of wood and berries. In 1875 the land came under the control of the Metropolitan Board of Works and, in 1996, the London Borough of Wandsworth. The commons now serve as green recreational space for the local community. The 128 hectares of land include a lido, a fishing lake, tennis courts, football and crickets pitches. Since the nineteenth century the commons have been divided by several intersecting railway lines.

3 Tooting Bec Lido

The Lido *(left)* is, at 91.5m long, the largest swimming pool and one of the oldest open-air pools in the UK. It opened in 1906 and was built as an initiative to get the local unemployed back to work. It is open to the public from May until September and to members for the whole year round.

Walking these pages: 6.4km

Falcon Brook

1 Northcote Road valley

Northcote Road runs along the bottom of a valley, beneath which Falcon Brook still flows. Adjoining streets to the east and the west all rise upwards towards the commons of Clapham and Wandsworth respectively. The road is an affluent shopping and restaurant area, popular with the locals of Battersea and Clapham, especially families. Consequently, it has earned the nickname of 'Nappy Valley'.

2 Arding & Hobbs

This department store was founded in nearby Wandsworth as a drapery shop. The original Battersea store, built in 1885, was badly damaged by a fire in 1909 in which nine people died. It was rebuilt *(right)* the following year, in an Edwardian Baroque style. Its size and appearance were to match and to compete with similar stores to be found in the West End. Although the name Arding & Hobbs is still displayed in large type on the corner of the store, it is now a part of the Debenhams chain.

3 The Falcon pub

There has been a pub on this site for over 300 years and it was named after the brook that once flowed openly past it. The pub sign depicts a rising golden falcon, a feature of the St John family crest. The St Johns were once the local lords of the manor who renamed the Hydeburn stream Falcon Brook. The current pub *(right)*, built in 1880, has the longest continuous bar in the UK and claims that the Dutch graphic artist M.C. Escher was involved in its design.

4 Clapham Junction

Clapham Junction, with its seventeen platforms, is reputed to be the busiest railway station in Europe. Of the 2,000 trains that pass through each day, 50 per cent stop here. It serves trains into and out of Victoria and Waterloo stations and onwards to numerous destinations to the south and west of London. Despite its name, the station is located in Battersea. It opened in 1863 and at the time the area contained factories and slum dwellings. The station owners, wanting to attract commuters, named the station Clapham (Junction), after the finer residential area 2km to the east.

Above: Looking west down into the Northcote Road valley. Above right: Arding & Hobbs department store. Right: The Falcon Brook's outfall into the Thames.

7 Price's candle factory

Located among the many foul-smelling industries along this stretch of the Thames during the Victorian era was Price's candle factory. The founders of the company had, in 1830, developed a method of extracting wax from cheap, raw materials such as coconuts and palm tree oil. The raw materials, initially from Sri Lanka, were brought up by barge to be crushed at the Battersea works before being sent back along the Thames to Vauxhall to be rendered into candles. By the end of the nineteenth century Price's had become the largest manufacturer of candles in the world, employing over 2,200 staff in their factories.

PRICE'S Hand Painted VENETIAN CANDLES

5 Falcon Brook splits just by Clapham Junction station. One branch flows west into the Thames close to York Road. The other branch follows the railway line towards Victoria and outfalls in the Thames to the east of Battersea Power Station.

6 Falconbrook Pumping Station

A pumping station on York Road was installed to protect the area close to the Thames from flooding during heavy rainfalls. During such rainstorms, water running off Streatham Hill can overwhelm the Victorian interceptor sewer and if the water and sewage is not quickly pumped into the Thames, it can inundate the low-lying areas. The introduction of the new Thames Tideway Tunnel will drastically reduce the risk of flooding.

Above left: The Falcon pub.
Above: A printed label for Price's Candles.

8 Battersea Creek Dock

By the mid-eighteenth century, factories had begun appearing along the Thames at Battersea. The marshy land was cheap and access to the river was vital for getting raw materials in and finished products out. Falcon Brook, where it flowed into the Thames, was developed as a tidal creek with facilities for barges to load and unload. Today the creek is no longer required and has been covered over. At low water on the Thames, the Falcon Brook outfall is visible in the mud *(left)*.

Falcon Brook

RIVER THAMES

York Road

YORK GARDENS

Bridges Crt Rd

London Heliport

Lavender Road

Darien Rd

Ingrave Street

Battersea Rise

St John's Hill

St John's Road

Falcon Road

Falcon Road

Falcon Road

Walking these pages: 3.2km

RIVER EFFRA

Complete walk 14.8km

The River Effra and its tributaries rise in the hills of Dulwich, Streatham and Sydenham. It flows north-north-westwards towards Vauxhall and the Thames. However, it is claimed that the river did not originally drain into the Thames where it does today but flowed eastwards across the marshes and flood plains of Walworth and Kennington, towards the Earl's Sluice, and drained into the Thames at Rotherhithe.

There are several theories about the origin of this river's unusual name. Possibly it is from the Old English word *efre* meaning 'bank' or the Celtic word *yfrid*, meaning 'torrent'.

The uncovered Effra was never wide nor deep enough to allow barges carrying raw materials even as far as Brixton and so consequently the area never developed as a manufacturing centre, unlike its upstream neighbour, Vauxhall.

By the mid-nineteenth century the Effra, with increasing urbanisation along its banks, was becoming an open sewer. Out of necessity, most of the river was culverted, with the exception of the Thames inlet at Vauxhall. And like most other central London rivers, it was press-ganged into service as part of the Bazalgette sewage network.

Left: The Crystal Palace transmitter.

3
At the end of the second cul-de-sac left off Hermitage Road is a drain cover. Here, at times, the Effra can be heard flowing below.

1 Crystal Palace

The area to the east of Westow Park is dominated by the Crystal Palace transmitter. This marks the location of the former Crystal Palace, designed by Joseph Paxton. The massive structure of iron and glass was created for the 1851 Great Exhibition in Hyde Park. The temporary exhibition building had, following the closure of the event, to be dismantled and moved. It was relocated to Penge Peak in 1854, and thus gave a new name to the area. The building was destroyed by fire in 1936.

2 Westow Park

This small park, 91m above sea level, is the main source of the Effra. Following a large amount of rainfall, the fenced-off ground at X can be very soggy. This is the point where the Effra springs out from between the clay and gravel on the hill. The stream immediately runs underground towards Harold Road.

Gipsy Hill station

Below: Crystal Palace bus terminal. Above: Virgo Fidelis Convent.

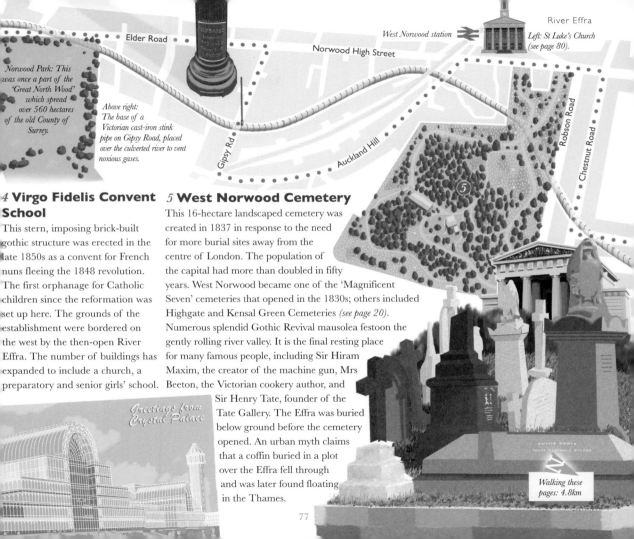

Elder Road

Norwood High Street

West Norwood station

River Effra

Left: St Luke's Church (see page 80).

Norwood Park: This was once a part of the 'Great North Wood' which spread over 560 hectares of the old County of Surrey.

Above right: The base of a Victorian cast-iron stink pipe on Gipsy Road, placed over the culverted river to vent noxious gases.

Gipsy Rd

Auckland Hill

Robson Road

Chestnut Road

⑤

4 Virgo Fidelis Convent School

This stern, imposing brick-built gothic structure was erected in the late 1850s as a convent for French nuns fleeing the 1848 revolution. The first orphanage for Catholic children since the reformation was set up here. The grounds of the establishment were bordered on the west by the then-open River Effra. The number of buildings has expanded to include a church, a preparatory and senior girls' school.

5 West Norwood Cemetery

This 16-hectare landscaped cemetery was created in 1837 in response to the need for more burial sites away from the centre of London. The population of the capital had more than doubled in fifty years. West Norwood became one of the 'Magnificent Seven' cemeteries that opened in the 1830s; others included Highgate and Kensal Green Cemeteries *(see page 20).* Numerous splendid Gothic Revival mausolea festoon the gently rolling river valley. It is the final resting place for many famous people, including Sir Hiram Maxim, the creator of the machine gun, Mrs Beeton, the Victorian cookery author, and Sir Henry Tate, founder of the Tate Gallery. The Effra was buried below ground before the cemetery opened. An urban myth claims that a coffin buried in a plot over the Effra fell through and was later found floating in the Thames.

Greetings from Crystal Palace

Walking these pages: 4.8km

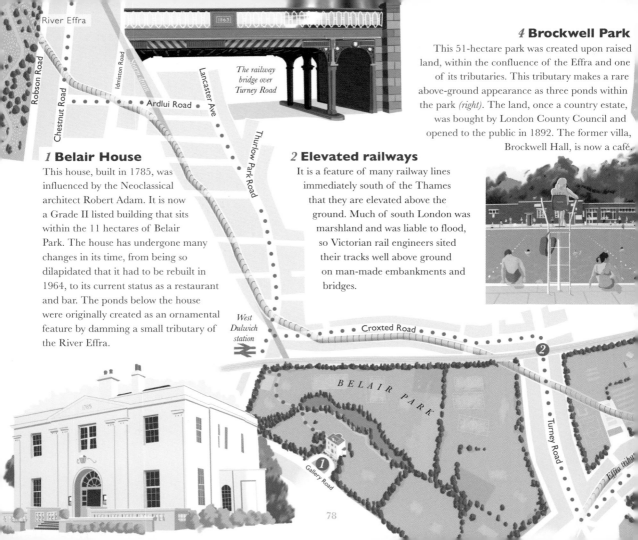

The railway bridge over Turney Road

4 Brockwell Park

This 51-hectare park was created upon raised land, within the confluence of the Effra and one of its tributaries. This tributary makes a rare above-ground appearance as three ponds within the park *(right)*. The land, once a country estate, was bought by London County Council and opened to the public in 1892. The former villa, Brockwell Hall, is now a café.

1 Belair House

This house, built in 1785, was influenced by the Neoclassical architect Robert Adam. It is now a Grade II listed building that sits within the 11 hectares of Belair Park. The house has undergone many changes in its time, from being so dilapidated that it had to be rebuilt in 1964, to its current status as a restaurant and bar. The ponds below the house were originally created as an ornamental feature by damming a small tributary of the River Effra.

2 Elevated railways

It is a feature of many railway lines immediately south of the Thames that they are elevated above the ground. Much of south London was marshland and was liable to flood, so Victorian rail engineers sited their tracks well above ground on man-made embankments and bridges.

River Effra

Effra tributary

Brixton Water Ln

Dalberg Road

Rattray Road

Jelf Rd

Saltoun Rd

Railton Rd

ponds

BROCKWELL PARK

4

5

Dulwich Road

Effra Parade

Herne Hill station

Half Moon Lane

Burbage Road

3

HERNE HILL VELODROME

5 Brockwell Lido

The lido *(left)* first opened in 1937, however it was forced to close in 1990 due to council budget cuts. It is now privately run, following its re-opening in 1994, and is accessible seven days a week, even during winter.

Right: Before the Effra was covered, houses along the Dulwich Road had small bridges to connect them with the thoroughfare.

John Ruskin

The art critic John Ruskin (1819–1900) *(right)* was brought up on Herne Hill. In his book *Praeterita*, he recalls his early life drawing the stream and fishing in it before it was culverted. By the 1840s, the river was becoming so polluted that those living nearby demanded it be covered over.

3 Herne Hill Velodrome

This open-air velodrome, tucked away off Burbage Road, was opened as a race track in 1891. During the inter-war years, up to 10,000 people would attend world championship events here. The velodrome was requisitioned as a barrage balloon depot during the Second World War and the track fell into disrepair. However, the banked cycle track was restored and became an internationally renowned venue during the London Olympics of 1948. Today, despite the tracks' exposure to the elements, it still is in use. A young Bradley Wiggins started racing here aged twelve.

Walking these pages: 6.1km

River Effra

2 St Matthew's Church

Following the population growth of the early nineteenth century, many new churches were needed in the expanding urban capital. St Matthew's was consecrated in 1824 and is the second* of three Commissioners' churches along the route of the Effra. The western portico features four large Greek Doric columns with the tower located at the opposite end. *St Luke's (see page 77) is the southernmost church on the Effra.*

4 Brixton Market

There has been a market in Brixton since the 1870s. It is now a hybrid of pedestrianised streets and covered arcades, many within the railway viaducts. As a community market, the traders sell fresh produce, hardware, clothing and accessories, with many cafés catering for all tastes. However, it is especially renowned for its African and Caribbean produce. Electric Avenue is so called as it was one of the first in the UK to be lit by electric illumination and, until the 1980s, featured a glazed roof. The arcades are now Grade II listed.

Brixton Hill ③

② Effra Road

Brixton Underground

Street markets
Covered markets

Electric Ave.

Electric Lane

④

Brixton Road

Gresham Road ⑥

⑤

⑦

Brixton Station Road

Brixton station

Coldharbour Lane

Atlantic Road

Rattray Rd ①

Kellett Road

Saltoun Rd

Brixton

In the 1860s, the village of Brixton was transformed into a London suburb by the arrival of the railways. It also became a major shopping centre of south London and by the 1920s boasted three department stores.

Following heavy bombing during the Second World War, much of the destroyed property was replaced with council houses. In 1948, newly arrived Caribbean immigrants sought work and settled in Brixton. It rapidly became popular with later arrivals and a multi-ethnic community developed over the next few decades. During five days in 1981, over 1,000 young black men were stopped and searched in Brixton, under the 'sus law'. In the riots which followed, over 300 were injured and many vehicles and properties were damaged.

1 Left: The Effra Hall Tavern sits immediately on the route of the river.

5 O₂ Academy Brixton

This Grade II listed Art Deco structure was designed in 1929 as a cinema, the Astoria, and survived as such until 1972. It then became a rock music venue, undergoing several name and ownership changes before being christened the Brixton Academy in 1983. Many famous bands have played here including The Sex Pistols, The Clash, Eric Clapton, Bob Dylan and The Smiths.

8 Vincent van Gogh

Between 1873 and 1874, the Dutch post-impressionist painter Vincent van Gogh lived at 87 Hackford Road while working for an art dealer in London. Van Gogh became infatuated with his landlady's daughter, Eugenie Loyer. After his proposal and her rejection of marriage, he distracted himself with long walks around London. In one of his letters home, he wrote: *'I walk here as much as I can. It's absolutely beautiful here.'*

River Effra

Hackford Road
8

Hillyard Street

GREATER LONDON COUNCIL
VINCENT
VAN
GOGH
1853-1890
Painter
lived here
1873-1874

Brixton Road

7 Max Roach Park

A series of dilapidated villas, whose front gardens overlaid the culverted Effra, were demolished to create a green space. The park was named after and opened by the famous American jazz drummer Max Roach in 1986. Roach performed and recorded with many jazz greats, including Miles Davis, Duke Ellington and Thelonius Monk.

6 Wooden water pipes

During building work in 1908, some wooden water pipes were unearthed in Gresham Road, just north of Brixton town centre. These sections of elm boughs *(above)*, each about a metre long, were bored out and fitted together. It is believed that these leaky conduits were carrying water from the Effra for drinking or irrigation purposes.

Right: The sculpture, by Raymond Wilson, is a memorial to the 116 children who died in the Soweto uprising in 1976. It is located within the Max Roach Park.

Walking these pages: 2.4km

3 Left: Brixton Town Hall, opened in 1908.

2 St Mark's Church

This is the third of the Commissioners' churches situated along the River Effra. It was consecrated in 1824. The interior was heavily damaged by bombing in 1940, and was restored by 1960.

Left: A Chartist handbill.
Above: St Mark's Church.
Right: The Oval cricket ground.

3 The Oval

The Oval has been home to Surrey County Cricket Club since 1845. A former tributary to the Effra *(shown as a blue dashed line below)* created an oval-shaped piece of land on which a market garden once stood. The area was prone to flooding. In 1880, spoil from excavating the enclosure of the Effra was used to create raised mounds for spectators. The ground became famous in 1870 for hosting the first England international football game. The match was played against Scotland and was a draw. The first FA Cup final was played here two years later. In 1882, Australia beat England in the first Test match to be held in the UK. The Oval is now invariably the location of the last Test match each summer.

1 Kennington Park

Prior to 1854, this park was known as Kennington Common, and it was here that around 150,000 Chartists gathered in April 1848 to hear speeches and to present a petition to Parliament. The Chartists were a working-class group demanding political reform and the vote for all men. The protest failed and universal male suffrage was not granted until 1918. In 1854 the common was converted into a green space for all within a burgeoning urban landscape.

River Effra

Brixton Road

Prima Road

Oval Underground

Kennington Oval

Camberwell New Rd

Harleyford St

Kennington Park Road

Former trib

Riverside industries

In the early nineteenth century, numerous industries were established along the banks of the Thames in Vauxhall and the Effra Creek. These included potteries, candle makers, tanneries and boat builders.

Many companies used the water as part of the production process and as a means of transporting finished goods away.

Right: Harleyford Road Community Gardens

6 Ancient pier

In the Thames, at very low water, wooden posts can be seen jutting out. These are the remains of a Bronze Age pier that was possibly used for ceremonial or funereal purposes.

Left: St George Wharf & Tower

Above: The storm relief sluice gate

Walking these pages: 1.7km

River Effra

Wandsworth Road

Lawn Lane

Langley Lane

Bonnington Square

Vauxhall Grove

Harleyford Road

South Lambert Road

S. Lambert Pl

Vauxhall Underground

Vauxhall station

Bridgefoot

Vauxhall Bridge

MI6 Building

RIVER THAMES

4 The Oval gas holders

There have been gas holders on this site since 1853. Originally designed to store coal gas produced on site, the holders have been decommissioned. However, they have become an integral part of the Oval's visual environment.

5 Vauxhall Pleasure Gardens

The pleasure gardens opened in 1660 and offered, to fee-paying customers, various entertainments, including music and dance, fireworks and trapeze artists. Handel's *Music for the Royal Fireworks* was previewed here, in 1749, to large crowds. Eventually the pleasure gardens became known as an area for vice, went into decline, and closed in 1859.

83

RIVER NECKINGER

Complete walk 6.0km

The River Neckinger does not rise on higher land to the south, as several of its neighbouring rivers do. Instead, it evolved in an area of south London marshland as a drainage ditch being fed by numerous smaller streams. It falls only a few metres before reaching the Thames.

The stream was formed both by nature and later by man-made efforts to channel water into powering industrial mills. The Neckinger's route runs eastwards to St Saviour's Dock, where it joined the Thames, although it is quite possible the Neckinger also drained northwards towards the South Bank. However, most of the river has been replaced or enhanced by storm drains and pumping stations that keep this lowland of south London free from flooding. The Neckinger's name is kept alive through street and building names.

Prior to the nineteenth century, those found guilty of pirateering or mutiny were hanged at a location close to the mouth of the Neckinger. The name of the river is derived from the hangman's neckerchief, or noose. On the opposite shore, at Wapping, those convicted by the British Admiralty were hanged and the bodies left for three tides to wash over them before being cut down.

Right: The Imperial War Museum with 15-inch naval guns that were installed in 1968.

Lambeth North Underground

Westminster Bridge Road

Morley College

King Edward Walk

Lambeth Road

Kennington Road

1 The Dog & Duck Tavern

The area around what is now Geraldine Mary Harmsworth Park was once known as St George's Fields. This was a much larger area consisting of marshland that was only traversable over raised causeways. Situated on Lambeth Road was The Dog & Duck Tavern, which took its name from the pastime of duck hunting with dogs. The tavern had a water spring within its grounds, and in 1731 the tavern was rebranded St George's Spa, as 'taking the waters' had become fashionable.

2 The Imperial War Museum

Not long after the St George's Spa closed, its grounds were acquired by Bethlem Royal Hospital of Moorfields. The institute for the insane needed more space and moved here in 1815. Just over a hundred years later the hospital moved again to its current location in Beckenham. The buildings and grounds were bought by Viscount Rothermere, who donated them to London County Council. The outer, patient wings were demolished to create more parkland. The idea to create a museum of war was put forward while the First World War was still in progress. Its role was to reflect and record the war effort by both military and civilian bodies of both the UK and the Commonwealth. After occupying two temporary sites the museum moved into its permanent home on Lambeth Road in 1936. The Imperial War Museum (IWM) houses a huge collection of military hardware, uniforms, photographs and ephemera from numerous fields of conflict. The buildings have been extensively refurbished and modernised over the past fifty years. Admission to the IWM is free.

3 Right: The Tibetan Peace Garden, sited within the Geraldine Mary Harmsworth Park, was opened in May 1999 by the Dalai Lama. The four-sided pillar carries a message of peace and harmony in four languages: Tibetan, Hindi, Chinese and English.

4 Left: A section of the Berlin Wall acquired by the Imperial War Museum in 1991. The Wall, originally erected in 1961, was designed to seal off East Germany from the West.

River Neckinger

CHANGE YOUR LiFE

5 Geraldine Mary Harmsworth Park

The former hospital and grounds were acquired by Harold Harmsworth, 1st Viscount Rothermere and newspaper proprietor, in 1930. He renamed the park after his mother and dedicated it to the *'splendid struggling mothers of Southwark and their children'*. Harmsworth was responsible for launching the *Daily Mail* and the *Daily Mirror*.

Geraldine Mary Harmsworth Park Opened 1934

Above right: Stone plaque on the Kennington Road entrance to Harmsworth Park.

Brook Drive · Austral St · Hayles St · Brook Drive · Elliott's Row · Oswin St · Pastor St · FP

Walking these pages: 1.9km

River Neckinger

1 The Michael Faraday Memorial

On the former traffic roundabout at Elephant and Castle sits a single-storey stainless-steel-panelled rectangular box. It is named the Michael Faraday Memorial and contains an electricity substation for the London Underground. It is a very apt tribute to the Victorian scientist who was born nearby in Newington Butts. Faraday discovered the principles of electromagnetic induction, which would lay the foundations for the creation of the electric motor.

Left: The Michael Faraday Memorial – a London Underground electricity substation. Below left: The Elephant and Castle sign outside the shopping centre.

3 The Rockingham Anomaly

Just off New Kent Road is a geological aberration known as the Rockingham Anomaly. It is a sunken peat bog that was formed during the last ice age. The Roman road Stane Street detoured from its straight line to avoid this damp hollow. The area has since been drained and built upon. However, a depression about 2m deep is still visible. Stand on Rockingham Street at the point where it makes a sharp turn (marked with an X) and observe all the roads running upwards.

Below: The former Heygate Estate.

2 Elephant and Castle

Elephant and Castle is situated at the south-eastern edge of what was St George's Fields, a former marshland. The Roman road Stane Street (now the A3) once passed through this location to avoid the quagmire. The district became a hub for six main roads and a coaching inn, The Elephant and Castle, which was established here in the sixteenth century, eventually christening the area. By the 1960s the confluence of the roads had become a major roundabout, which would dominate the area along with new high-rise buildings and the first covered shopping centre in Europe. Most of these have since gone into decline. A major redevelopment of housing, roads, office and retail space is underway to improve the area.

5 Hartley's jam factory

Hartley's first started producing jams and marmalades in Lancashire in 1871. The company grew rapidly and in 1902 they opened a new preserve factory in Bermondsey. The district became home to many well-known household brands, including Peek Frean biscuits, Crosse & Blackwell and Sarson's vinegar. Proximity to the Thames and the rail hub enabled rapid access for getting raw materials in and finished products out. The factory has now been converted into residential apartments. In an attempt to rebrand the area, estate agents created the term SoBo – South of Borough. The term never caught on.

Above: The former Hartley's factory, now residential apartments. Right: A ceramic Hartley's marmalade pot.

Right: St Mary Magdalene on Bermondsey Street.

River Neckinger

St Mary Magdalene Church and churchyard

6 Bermondsey Abbey

In 1082, a Cluniac priory was established upon a gravel outcrop or eyot, within the Thames floodplain known as Beormund Eyot. The monastery was located adjacent to the Neckinger. The nave of the abbey ran along what is now Abbey Street. Over the next few centuries the monastery acquired more land and influence. They created a dock, St Saviour's, where the Neckinger entered the Thames and they rerouted the stream to power water mills and drain marshland. Following the schism with Rome, Henry VIII began the Dissolution of the Monasteries in 1536. The abbey's estate was sold off and its buildings destroyed. Nothing remains of the abbey today. The medieval church of St Mary Magdalene now stands just north of the abbey grounds. It was rebuilt in 1830 in a Gothic Revival style.

4 Heygate Estate

This was the site of a former large social housing estate that opened in 1974. The brutalist concrete construction was home to around 3,000 people and it was claimed engendered no sense of community and eventually developed a reputation for crime and poverty. In its later years it became a location for film makers seeking a decaying urban backdrop. In 2014 the estate was demolished and handed over to private developers to build new apartments and houses with some being offered at 'affordable' prices.

Walking these pages: 2.3km

Bermondsey leather industry

The area of Bermondsey around the abbey became heavily involved in the manufacture of leather along with related industries of dyeing and finishing. This initially started in the medieval era when several of the abbey's adjacent farms on Grange Road and Grange Walk were given over to leather production. Vital to the process of animal skin preparation was water. The Neckinger, which was then tidal to this point in Bermondsey, was able to replenish stocks twice each day. Some fairly noxious materials were used in the production of leather, including dog and pigeon fæces and human urine. Consequently, the whole area stank, especially in warmer weather. The leather industry grew with the nineteenth-century population boom and the area became the largest producer of leather in Europe. However, production declined over the twentieth century and had ceased entirely by 1990.

Local thoroughfares such as Tanner Street, Leathermarket Street and Morocco Street still recall the former industry of the area.

TANNER STREET SE1
LONDON BOROUGH OF SOUTHWARK

Above: A Victorian leather craftsman prepares a hide.

5 St Saviour's Dock

This dock was once the point at which the Neckinger flowed into the Thames. Under the direction of the monks of Bermondsey Abbey, the inlet was enlarged to enable ships and barges to tie up alongside the docks to make unloading and loading more efficient. The dock was named after the abbey's patron saint. The Neckinger was rerouted eastwards to create a reservoir to power a tidal mill and created what was became known as Jacob's Island. Over the past thirty years, the former Victorian warehouses have been converted into offices and residential apartments.

1 Abbey Street Railway Bridge. The central section of this bridge was part of the London and Greenwich Railway. It opened in 1836 and was the first railway line in the capital.

Grange Walk

The Grange

Grange Walk

Neckinger

2 Bevington's Neckinger Mills

The Quaker Bevington family established a leather production factory and warehouse on Abbey Street, close to the Neckinger, in 1795. Previously there had been a paper manufacturer on the site that also exploited the adjacent water supply in its production. A member of the family, Samuel Bourne Bevington, became the first Mayor of Bermondsey in 1900. The former warehouse is now residential apartments.

NECKINGER MILLS
BEVINGTON & SONS

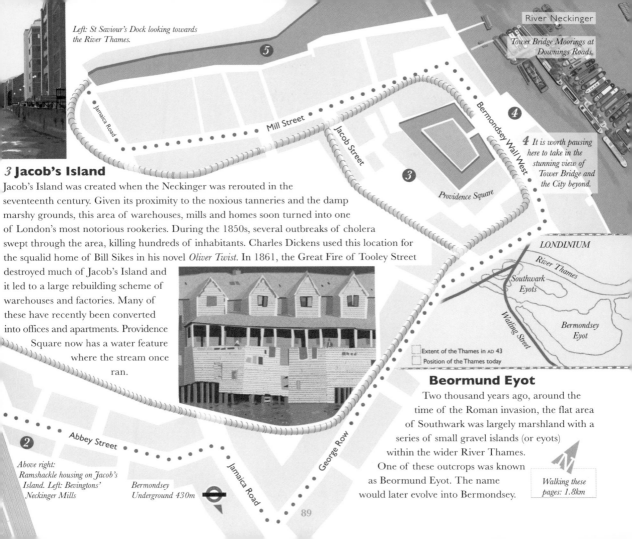

Left: St Saviour's Dock looking towards the River Thames.

River Neckinger

Tower Bridge Moorings at Downings Roads.

3 Jacob's Island

Jacob's Island was created when the Neckinger was rerouted in the seventeenth century. Given its proximity to the noxious tanneries and the damp marshy grounds, this area of warehouses, mills and homes soon turned into one of London's most notorious rookeries. During the 1850s, several outbreaks of cholera swept through the area, killing hundreds of inhabitants. Charles Dickens used this location for the squalid home of Bill Sikes in his novel *Oliver Twist*. In 1861, the Great Fire of Tooley Street destroyed much of Jacob's Island and it led to a large rebuilding scheme of warehouses and factories. Many of these have recently been converted into offices and apartments. Providence Square now has a water feature where the stream once ran.

4 It is worth pausing here to take in the stunning view of Tower Bridge and the City beyond.

LONDINIUM

River Thames

Southwark Eyots

Watling Street

Bermondsey Eyot

Extent of the Thames in AD 43
Position of the Thames today

Beormund Eyot

Two thousand years ago, around the time of the Roman invasion, the flat area of Southwark was largely marshland with a series of small gravel islands (or eyots) within the wider River Thames. One of these outcrops was known as Beormund Eyot. The name would later evolve into Bermondsey.

Above right: Ramshackle housing on Jacob's Island. Left: Bevingtons' Neckinger Mills

Bermondsey Underground 430m

Walking these pages: 1.8km

EARL'S SLUICE

Complete walk 9.9km

The Earl's Sluice rises in what is now a duck pond in Ruskin Park, Denmark Hill. It descends northwards on to the south London lowlands, where it acts, in conjunction with other streams, as a drainage channel. The sluice takes its name from the twelfth-century William FitzRobert, Lord of the Manor of Camberwell and Peckham and Earl of Gloucester. He was an illegitimate son of Henry I.

It is believed that the River Effra (see page 76) once flowed eastwards from the Oval to join the Earl's Sluice. Monks of Bermondsey Priory rerouted the Effra into the Thames at Vauxhall to enable the flatlands of Walworth and Bermondsey to dry out and become more agriculturally productive.

By the 1820s much of the sluice was covered over to allow housing to be built above. It became known as the Earl Main Sewer and during the 1870s it was commandeered into the Metropolitan Board of Works sewerage system for London. At times of heavy and sudden downfalls, the pumping station, on Chilton Grove, has to clear water directly into the Thames.

The sluice acts as a natural boundary between the areas of Bermondsey/Rotherhithe and Camberwell/Deptford, and once formed part of the old county line between Kent and Surrey.

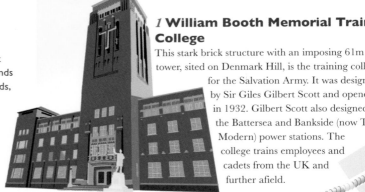

1 William Booth Memorial Training College

This stark brick structure with an imposing 61m tower, sited on Denmark Hill, is the training college for the Salvation Army. It was designed by Sir Giles Gilbert Scott and opened in 1932. Gilbert Scott also designed the Battersea and Bankside (now Tate Modern) power stations. The college trains employees and cadets from the UK and further afield.

Above: The William Booth Memorial Training College with a statue of the founder, William Booth.

Right: The bandstand in Ruskin Park.

Left: The Portico.

2 The Portico

Ruskin Park was built over a series of large properties and gardens that lined Denmark Hill. One of the porticos has been preserved within the park as a shelter.

90

4 King's College Hospital

The hospital was founded in 1840, just south of Lincoln's Inn Fields, where it had established itself as a medical training facility within the rookeries of Aldwych. By the end of the nineteenth century the population of the area had declined and the hospital was moved, in 1913, to a green field site on Denmark Hill. Over the past hundred years new buildings and facilities have been added. It is now an NHS Foundation Trust that serves a large area of south London.

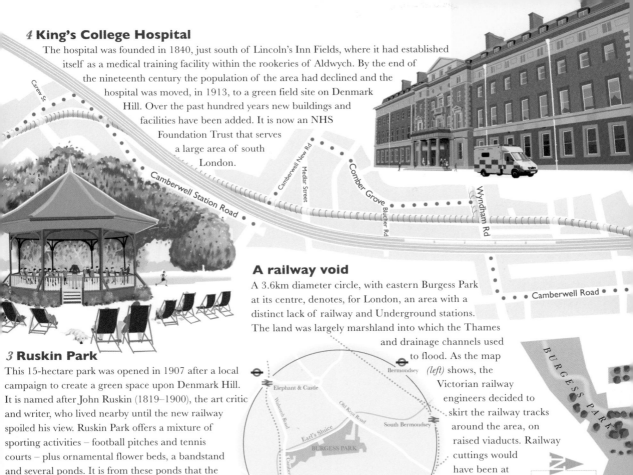

Carew St

Camberwell Station Road

Camberwell New Rd

Medlar Street

Comber Grove

Blucher Rd

Wyndham Rd

Camberwell Road

A railway void

A 3.6km diameter circle, with eastern Burgess Park at its centre, denotes, for London, an area with a distinct lack of railway and Underground stations. The land was largely marshland into which the Thames and drainage channels used to flood. As the map *(left)* shows, the Victorian railway engineers decided to skirt the railway tracks around the area, on raised viaducts. Railway cuttings would have been at great risk of flooding.

Bermondsey

Elephant & Castle

Walworth Road

Old Kent Road

South Bermondsey

Earl's Sluice

BURGESS PARK

Camberwell Road

Peckham Road

Queen's Road

Peckham Ryr.

BURGESS PARK

Walking these pages: 3.0km

3 Ruskin Park

This 15-hectare park was opened in 1907 after a local campaign to create a green space upon Denmark Hill. It is named after John Ruskin (1819–1900), the art critic and writer, who lived nearby until the new railway spoiled his view. Ruskin Park offers a mixture of sporting activities – football pitches and tennis courts – plus ornamental flower beds, a bandstand and several ponds. It is from these ponds that the Earl's Sluice rises and flows northwards underground towards the hospital and Camberwell.

91

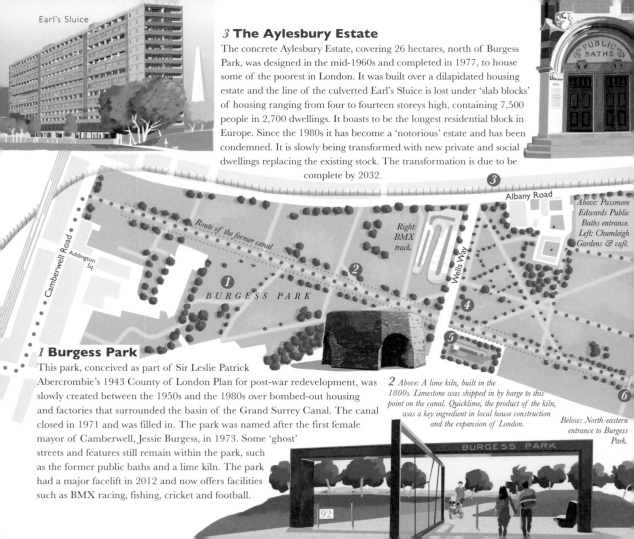

3 The Aylesbury Estate

The concrete Aylesbury Estate, covering 26 hectares, north of Burgess Park, was designed in the mid-1960s and completed in 1977, to house some of the poorest in London. It was built over a dilapidated housing estate and the line of the culverted Earl's Sluice is lost under 'slab blocks' of housing ranging from four to fourteen storeys high, containing 7,500 people in 2,700 dwellings. It boasts to be the longest residential block in Europe. Since the 1980s it has become a 'notorious' estate and has been condemned. It is slowly being transformed with new private and social dwellings replacing the existing stock. The transformation is due to be complete by 2032.

Above: Passmore Edwards Public Baths entrance. Left: Chumleigh Gardens & café.

1 Burgess Park

This park, conceived as part of Sir Leslie Patrick Abercrombie's 1943 County of London Plan for post-war redevelopment, was slowly created between the 1950s and the 1980s over bombed-out housing and factories that surrounded the basin of the Grand Surrey Canal. The canal closed in 1971 and was filled in. The park was named after the first female mayor of Camberwell, Jessie Burgess, in 1973. Some 'ghost' streets and features still remain within the park, such as the former public baths and a lime kiln. The park had a major facelift in 2012 and now offers facilities such as BMX racing, fishing, cricket and football.

2 Above: A lime kiln, built in the 1800s. Limestone was shipped in by barge to this point on the canal. Quicklime, the product of the kiln, was a key ingredient in local house construction and the expansion of London.

Below: North-eastern entrance to Burgess Park.

Earl's Sluice

Camberwell Road

Addington Sq

Route of the former canal

BURGESS PARK

Right: BMX track.

Wells Way

Albany Road

BURGESS PARK

92

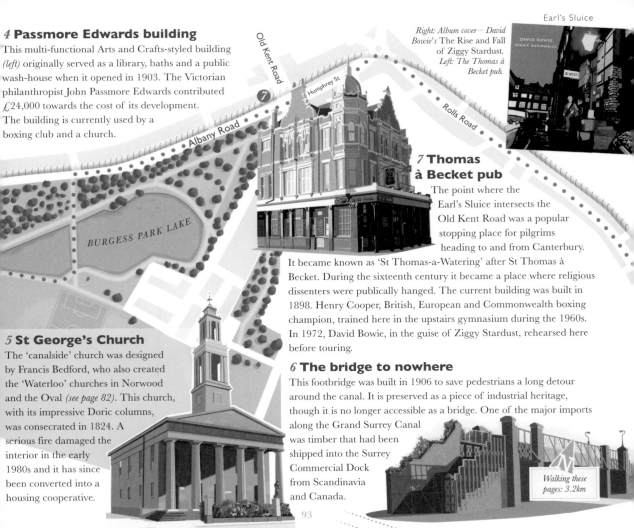

4 Passmore Edwards building

This multi-functional Arts and Crafts-styled building *(left)* originally served as a library, baths and a public wash-house when it opened in 1903. The Victorian philanthropist John Passmore Edwards contributed £24,000 towards the cost of its development. The building is currently used by a boxing club and a church.

Right: Album cover – David Bowie's The Rise and Fall of Ziggy Stardust.
Left: The Thomas à Becket pub.

Earl's Sluice

7 Thomas à Becket pub

The point where the Earl's Sluice intersects the Old Kent Road was a popular stopping place for pilgrims heading to and from Canterbury. It became known as 'St Thomas-a-Watering' after St Thomas à Becket. During the sixteenth century it became a place where religious dissenters were publically hanged. The current building was built in 1898. Henry Cooper, British, European and Commonwealth boxing champion, trained here in the upstairs gymnasium during the 1960s. In 1972, David Bowie, in the guise of Ziggy Stardust, rehearsed here before touring.

5 St George's Church

The 'canalside' church was designed by Francis Bedford, who also created the 'Waterloo' churches in Norwood and the Oval *(see page 82)*. This church, with its impressive Doric columns, was consecrated in 1824. A serious fire damaged the interior in the early 1980s and it has since been converted into a housing cooperative.

6 The bridge to nowhere

This footbridge was built in 1906 to save pedestrians a long detour around the canal. It is preserved as a piece of industrial heritage, though it is no longer accessible as a bridge. One of the major imports along the Grand Surrey Canal was timber that had been shipped into the Surrey Commercial Dock from Scandinavia and Canada.

Walking these pages: 3.2km

1 Southern Railway Stables

On the corner of Catlin Street and St James's Road is the Southern Railway Stables *(right)*. This would appear to be an odd urban location for such a facility. However, the stable was founded here in the mid-nineteenth century for the then-adjacent Bricklayers' Arms railway station and depot (the marshalling yards and tracks were

located to the north of Rolls Road). Working horses from the station were stabled and cared for here. Though the station and track no longer exist, the stables continue to function today for recreational horses.

2 The rivers merge

The Earl's Creek and the River Peck *(see page 96)* merge at this point to form the Earl Main Sewer. This sewer was created in the early 1800s to facilitate better drainage of the surrounding marshlands.

4 The Earl Pumping Station

This pumping station works to prevent the local area from flooding. After moderate rainfall, most of the water is sent eastwards to the Crossness treatment plant in Thamesmead. However, after heavy downpours the Victorian system cannot cope and untreated sewage has to be pumped into the Thames nearby. The planned Thames Tideway 'super-sewer' will greatly reduce the number of discharges into the river.

Right: The Earl Pumping Station.

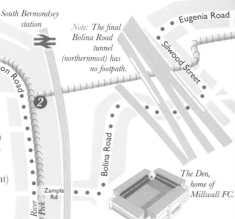

Note: The final Bolina Road tunnel (northernmost) has no footpath.

The Den, home of Millwall FC.

3 River over rail

By Oldfield Grove, close to Rotherhithe New Road, there is a single pipe *(left)*, about 60cm in diameter, that straddles the railway cutting. This conduit carries the Earl's Sluice (named Earl Main Sewer by this point) over the railway line.

5 Greenland and South Docks

These two stretches of water were once part of a much larger group of man-made inland docks, collectively known as the Surrey Commercial Docks (SCD). The Howland Great Wet Dock opened in 1700 and was London's first inland dock, capable of holding 120 merchant vessels. Within twenty years, the dock was being used mainly by Greenland whaling ships and was renamed the Greenland Dock. The South Dock was drained during the Second World War and used to construct temporary (Mulberry) harbours for use in the D-Day landings. With the rise of containerisation in the 1960s, the SCD went into decline and closed. The London Dockland Development Corporation, tasked with redeveloping the entire London Docklands, filled in nearly all of the SCD. But Greenland and South Docks were preserved as a marina and for watersports.

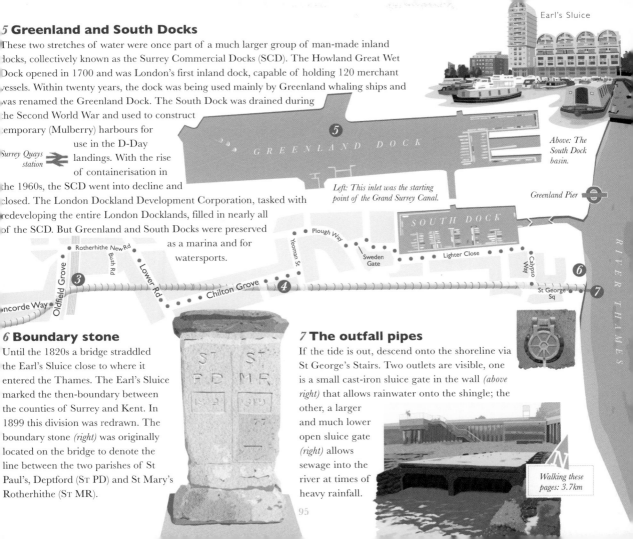

Earl's Sluice

Above: The South Dock basin.

Left: This inlet was the starting point of the Grand Surrey Canal.

Greenland Pier

Surrey Quays station

GREENLAND DOCK

SOUTH DOCK

RIVER THAMES

Rotherhithe New Rd · Bush Rd · Lower Rd · Oldfield Grove · Concorde Way · Chilton Grove · Yeoman St · Plough Way · Sweden Gate · Lighter Close · Calypso Way · St George Sq

Walking these pages: 3.7km

6 Boundary stone

Until the 1820s a bridge straddled the Earl's Sluice close to where it entered the Thames. The Earl's Sluice marked the then-boundary between the counties of Surrey and Kent. In 1899 this division was redrawn. The boundary stone *(right)* was originally located on the bridge to denote the line between the two parishes of St Paul's, Deptford (ST PD) and St Mary's Rotherhithe (ST MR).

ST PD · ST MR · 77

7 The outfall pipes

If the tide is out, descend onto the shoreline via St George's Stairs. Two outlets are visible, one is a small cast-iron sluice gate in the wall *(above right)* that allows rainwater onto the shingle; the other, a larger and much lower open sluice gate *(right)* allows sewage into the river at times of heavy rainfall.

RIVER PECK

Complete walk 7.4km

The River Peck rises on a small wooded hill in south-east London and flows roughly northwards to join the Earl's Sluice before it enters the Thames at Rotherhithe. The river gave its name to one of the villages it passes through: Peckham – the village (ham) by the River Peck.

Unlike many other London rivers, the Peck was not heavily polluted in the upper reaches and consequently it is visible for over half a kilometre as it traverses Peckham Rye Park.

The term stream, rather than river, must apply to it here, for it is only about a metre wide. Once beyond the park the Peck becomes subterranean again.

The walk, following the route of the Peck from rural Honor Oak Park to South Bermondsey, passes through parkland, common, urban industrial and housing estates on its way to join the Earl's Sluice.

This is a journey of many contrasts, as it passes a former prisoner-of-war camp, the location where William Blake witnessed one of his first visions, a former lido that may one day take its water from the Peck, the grand portico of Caroline Gardens, and the home of Millwall Football Club. It ends where the Peck meets the Earl's Sluice.

Note: The path up to and down One Tree Hill, consists of large, uneven concrete steps.

Honor Oak Park

Honor Oak Park

Honor Oak Park Overground

1 St Augustine's Church

St Augustine's Church is located on the eastern side of One Tree Hill, within Honor Oak Park, and is part of the Diocese of Southwark. It was consecrated in 1872 and is built of Kentish ragstone. The tower was added some sixteen years later and the church is now a Grade II listed building.

2 Gun emplacement

One Tree Hill is 92m above sea level and as such it has been used as a telegraph signal post for the military during the Napoleonic Wars and by the East India Company. The battered-looking concrete-and-brick hexagonal plinth was created during the First World War. It housed a naval gun used to counter attacks by German Zeppelins. The beacon immediately adjacent to the platform was constructed to celebrate the coronation of Queen Elizabeth II in 1953.

3 Left: The view over London from the top of One Tree Hill.

4 The Oak of Honor

It has been claimed that Queen Elizabeth I may have rested under this tree's predecessor *(above left)* on May Day in 1602. It became known thereafter as the 'Oak of Honor'. The tree lasted until 1888 and was replaced in 1905. This is the 'one tree' of One Tree Hill and it once formed part of the Great North Wood *(see page 77)*. From the reign of William I until Queen Victoria, these managed woods provided timber for ship building yards in Deptford, 4km away.

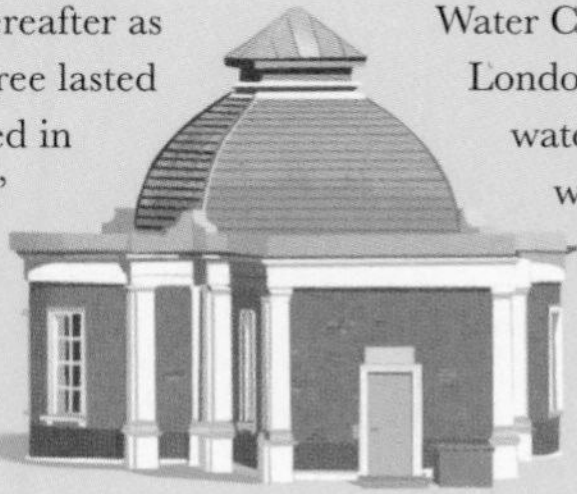

6 Honor Oak Reservoir

Beneath this 12-hectare area of grass with a nine-hole golf course is a water reservoir. It was built between 1901 and 1909, by the Southwark and Vauxhall Water Company, to supply the south-east of London with clean water. This brick-built water store was the largest of its type in the world and could hold up to 270,000m³ of water. The bricks used to construct the labyrinthine reservoir were created from the clay excavated from within the site. It is now a part of the Thames Water Ring Main. The River Peck flows below the reservoir but does not feed into it.

Above: A drained section of the Honor Oak Reservoir. Far left: An entrance into the reservoir.

The grass cover of the reservoir is used by the Aquarius Golf Club.

Brenchley Gardens

CAMBERWELL NEW CEMETERY

Kelvington Road

Cheltenham Road

5 A few metres into Kelvington Road, observe the raised embankments to the left and right of the road. This is the remains of the Nunhead to Crystal Palace High Level Railway line. It closed in the mid-1950s.

Walking these pages: 1.4km

River Peck

1 Ornamental gardens

Peckham Rye Park was opened to the public in 1894 complete with an 'Old English Garden'. This was later named the Sexby Garden, after London County Council's first Chief Officer of Parks. A network of pergolas, centred around a fountain, are populated with mature shrubs and plants. A Japanese garden was created in 1908, located close to the Sexby Garden. The shelter was added in 2005.

Above: The River Peck as it enters Peckham Rye Park.

4 The Peck grate

Just before the River Peck leaves Peckham Rye Park it heads back underground. The only indication of it on the Common are two manhole covers. Sometimes the river can be heard below.

Note: The trail marked here, across P

PECKHAM RYE COMMON

Peckham Rye

2 The Peck in the Park

Most of London's hidden rivers rarely reveal themselves until very close to the Thames, if at all. The River Peck makes an appearance for over half a kilometre as it flows through Peckham Rye Park. It has been landscaped into the park as a feature but it follows the original course the Peck used to take.

The Lake

Peckham Rye

3 Prisoner-of-war camp

During the Second World War a prisoner-of-war camp was built on Peckham Rye Common to house captured Italian soldiers. The POWs were given the task of raising chickens and pigs and growing vegetables on the common. One of the huts still remains *(left)* and is used as a pre-school club.

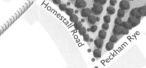

Homestall Road

Peckham Rye

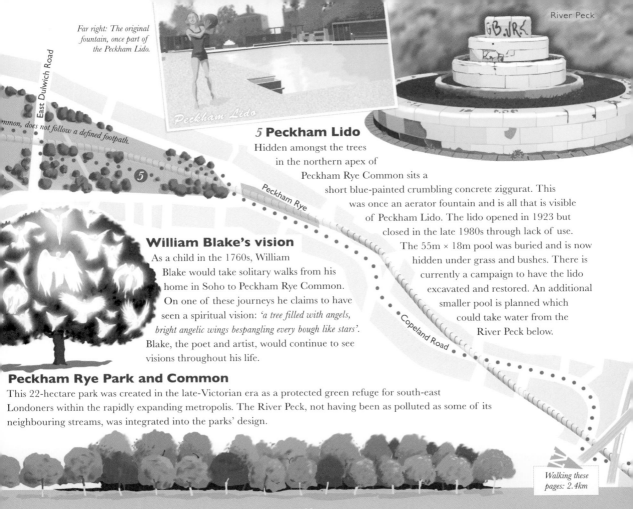

Far right: The original fountain, once part of the Peckham Lido.

Peckham Lido

5 Peckham Lido

Hidden amongst the trees
in the northern apex of
Peckham Rye Common sits a
short blue-painted crumbling concrete ziggurat. This
was once an aerator fountain and is all that is visible
of Peckham Lido. The lido opened in 1923 but
closed in the late 1980s through lack of use.
The 55m × 18m pool was buried and is now
hidden under grass and bushes. There is
currently a campaign to have the lido
excavated and restored. An additional
smaller pool is planned which
could take water from the
River Peck below.

East Dulwich Road

mmon, does not follow a defined footpath.

Peckham Rye

Copeland Road

William Blake's vision

As a child in the 1760s, William
Blake would take solitary walks from his
home in Soho to Peckham Rye Common.
On one of these journeys he claims to have
seen a spiritual vision: *'a tree filled with angels,
bright angelic wings bespangling every bough like stars'*.
Blake, the poet and artist, would continue to see
visions throughout his life.

Peckham Rye Park and Common

This 22-hectare park was created in the late-Victorian era as a protected green refuge for south-east
Londoners within the rapidly expanding metropolis. The River Peck, not having been as polluted as some of its
neighbouring streams, was integrated into the parks' design.

*Walking these
pages: 2.4km*

On to the flood plain

Once the River Peck has passed beyond Peckham Rye Common it enters what was once the former flood plains of south London. If there ever was a detectable river valley in this flat land, then part of it, along Ilderton Road, has been usurped by a railway line with the river flowing beneath the tracks towards the Earl's Sluice in South Bermondsey.

3 Clifton Terrace

Clifton Terrace is a single row of two- and three-storey houses that were built between 1846 and 1850. These red-brick houses *(above)*, with their belated Regency styling, without stucco, could have been relocated from Brighton.

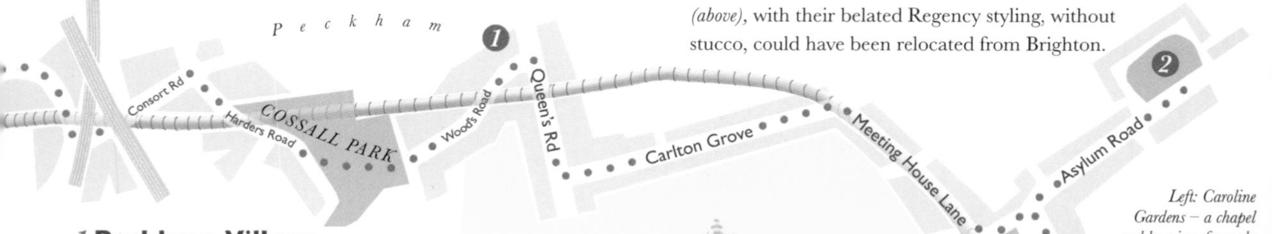

Left: Caroline Gardens – a chapel and housing, formerly retirement homes for pub landlords and ladies.

1 Peckham Village

Before 1800, Peckham was a village beyond London, surrounded by market gardens. Along Queen's Road are numerous fine examples of early-eighteenth-century housing that still stand despite the ravages of urban development. The example shown below, set back on the corner of Queen's Road and Wood's Road, was built around 1700.

2 Caroline Gardens

Set back off Asylum Road is a grass courtyard lined with impressive almshouses and a chapel within 2.5 hectares of land. These were built in 1827 by the Licensed Victuallers' Benevolent Institute, as a home for retired publicans of the area. Following bomb damage during the Second World War, the LVBI sold the site to the London Borough of Southwark and it is now used as social housing. It was renamed Caroline Gardens, after a former resident, Caroline Secker, widow of Marine Sergeant James Secker, who carried Admiral Nelson below deck following his fall at the Battle of Trafalgar.

4 The many houses of God

Dotted amongst the builders' warehouses and industrial parks along Ilderton Road are a large selection of evangelical and other non-conformist churches.

5 The Grand Surrey Canal

The canal, it was proposed, would link the Thames and Surrey Commercial Docks at Rotherhithe with Kingston in Surrey. It opened in 1807, but the funds to build it were diverted into the more profitable docks and the canal only reached as far as Camberwell. The canal closed following the demise of the docks in the early 1970s and was later filled in and partially converted into a road. The prefixed title of 'Grand' is rather misleading.

Below: The Grand Surrey Canal c.1900.

6 The New Den

The Den is home to the Millwall Football Club. They were formed as a canning factory workers' team in Millwall, on the Isle of Dogs, in 1885. Having moved grounds several times they relocated to New Cross, south London in 1910, while still retaining the name Millwall. During the late 1980s, the team gained promotion to what was then still Division One and the need for a new larger, all-seater ground arose. They moved to the New Den, South Bermondsey, in 1993, though the team later dropped back down through the divisions.

Above: Millwall FC ground.

Zampa Road

Bolina Road

Silwood St

Eugenia Road

Ilderton Road

Route of former Grand Surrey Canal

7 Railway arches

As a result of Victorian railway mania, numerous lines were built in parallel, as can be witnessed here (right). Five pairs of railway lines have to be passed under to reach the far side. Be warned, the last or northernmost tunnel has no footpath.

8 The Earl's Sluice

The River Peck meets the Earl's Sluice at this point and flows eastwards to the Thames (see page 94).

Walking these pages: 3.6km

SIR JOSEPH BAZALGETTE

The great Victorian engineer whose grand masterplan press-ganged many Thames tributaries into becoming sewers.

In 1650, the population of London was about 350,000. Two hundred years later this figure had increased sevenfold to 2,360,000. Despite this, the system for clearing sewage had not changed much. No network of sewage pipes had been implemented and the 'nightmen', with their horses and carts, would still empty the cesspits. The removed ordure was usually treated and converted into fertiliser. Sometimes, however, the sewage was simply dumped into the nearest river.

The rivers and streams that fed into the Thames were also being used to deposit many other kinds of unwanted matter. Chemicals and urine used in the processing of leather, blood and gore from Smithfield Market, as well as industrial detritus, were all being dumped into the nearest waterway. Dead animals and human corpses could end up here too. Despite Parliamentary legislation ordering those with properties adjacent to the rivers and streams to keep them clear and free-flowing, this was often ignored and waterways would clog up and become stagnant. The once-clean rivers and streams began to smell foul, with the waters no longer safe to drink.

The solution to this problem was a simple one: just cover the stinking rivers over. This process of culverting started in the eighteenth century and was completed by the 1870s. However, the sewage problem was merely being shifted down into the Thames.

The Great Stink

In 1849, over 14,000 Londoners died in a cholera epidemic. This was one of several that had struck the capital in the first half of the nineteenth century. At the time it was commonly believed that the infection was airborne. However, Dr John Snow, an early epidemiologist, began studying the outbreak of cholera in 1849. His maps, detailing the geographical spread of the disease, led him to conclude that it was transmitted by water. Dr Snow revealed that a water pump in Broad Street (now Broadwick Street), Soho, was the source of the local outbreak. The pump was only a metre away from a leaky cesspit.

In 1858, the year of the 'Great Stink', Parliament was forced to abandon sittings in the Commons, as the stench from the adjacent Thames had become too great to endure. Accumulated sewage on the river now formed a thick, rancid sludge and was decomposing in the summer heat. Two years earlier, Parliament had passed an Act that established the Metropolitan Board of Works, with the sole aim of overhauling the sewage system of London. However, the Great Stink focussed the minds of the MPs into urging greater and faster action from the Board of Works.

The Interceptor Sewers

Joseph Bazalgette, born in Enfield in 1819, was appointed chief engineer to the Metropolitan Board of Works. His plan was to create a network of 160km of large brick-built interceptor sewers that would run from west to east. These would be fed into by 725km of new smaller sewers and also by the culverted rivers and streams plus hundreds of smaller old local sewers and drains. All sewage and rainwater would now be removed to treatment plants to the east of London. Two sewage works were created: one in Beckton on the north of the river and one in Crossness on the south side. The treated sewage was to be flushed into the Thames on the ebb tide, thus, in theory, sending it out into the estuary and the sea.

Bazalgette and his team of engineers narrowed parts of the Thames in central London to improve the tidal flow and flush the river more efficiently. In 1864 work began to create the Victoria Embankment between Westminster and Blackfriars. A new shoreline was created, reducing the width of the river by up to 130m in places, using massive granite blocks. The new Victoria Embankment not only carried one of the main interceptor sewers, it also included an underground railway line (later known as the Circle and District lines) and a new public garden was created above the train lines and sewer. Further Thames-narrowing embankments were also created at Vauxhall and Chelsea.

Bazalgette, not content with creating a massive sewage system for London, also designed several bridges over the Thames, including Putney Bridge (1886), Battersea Bridge (1887) and Hammersmith Bridge (1890). He was also involved with the initial plans for the Blackwall Tunnel. Joseph Bazalgette was knighted for his

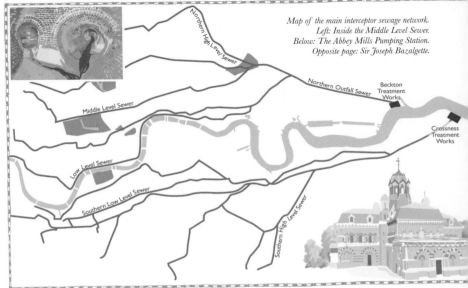

Map of the main interceptor sewage network.
Left: Inside the Middle Level Sewer.
Below: The Abbey Mills Pumping Station.
Opposite page: Sir Joseph Bazalgette.

services to engineering and public health in 1875 and died in 1891.

Thames Tideway Tunnel

Today, during periods of heavy rainfall, the sewage system cannot cope with the volume, so rainwater combined with sewage has to be discharged into the Thames, otherwise it would back up into streets and houses. The Victorian interceptor sewers were designed for a population of four million people. Today the population of London is over eight

million and rising and the sewer network, at times, becomes overloaded. On average nearly 40,000,000m^3 of rainwater and sewage enters the Thames each year.

By the late twentieth century it was clear that a major overhaul of the network was required. Following consultation and planning, a new 25km interceptor tunnel is being built 70m under the Thames to carry sewage to the treatment plant at Beckton. When completed in 2023, it will drastically reduce the amount of raw sewage that enters the Thames.

ACKNOWLEDGEMENTS

In walking and researching London's Hidden Rivers, I've worked with numerous people and friends who have assisted me in creating this book. My sincere thanks to the following: ∾ Rob Smith for pointing out Lenin's love of fish and chip suppers ∾ The guides Jenni Bowley and Rhona Levene of Footprint of London ∾ Natalia Kornioukhova for her Russian translation ∾ Martin Knight for sharing his knowledge of the upper River Effra ∾ Martin Stanley's tour of the low lands of Vauxhall and Lambeth and a possible earlier route of the River Effra ∾ Stephen Brown of Kensal Green Cemetery ∾ Henry Vivian-Neal, trustee of the Friends of Kensal Green Cemetery for revealing the 'hidden' well ∾ Steve Crow, Jeff Gerhardt, Jeremy Smith and staff of the London Metropolitan Archive ∾ Tom Simpson, Abney Park Cemetery manager ∾ Ken Wilson for supplying details on Brook Type ∾ Bill Bailey, chairman of the Hanger Hill Garden Estate Residents Association ∾ Chris Dane (also for his Arsenal FC contribution), Jules Taylor, Michael Court and Yuko Yamaguchi for walking various sections of the hidden rivers with me and checking my maps and details ∾ The web based maps of Open Street, Bing, Apple and Google ∾ My agent, Sheila Ableman ∾ And finally thanks to my wife, Sheila Fathers, for proofing all my copy (and walking and checking several of the rivers too).

BIBLIOGRAPHY

Author(s)	Title	Publisher	Year
Ackroyd, Peter	London Under	Vintage	2012
Barton, Nicholas & Myers, Stephen	The Lost Rivers of London	Historical Publications	2016
Bolton, Tom	London's Lost River	Strange Attractor Press	2011
Beames, Thomas	The Rookeries of London	Dodo Press	2009
Bradley, Simon & Pevsner, Nikolaus	London 1: The City of London	Penguin	1999
Bradley, Simon & Pevsner, Nikolaus	London 6: Westminster	Yale University Press	2005
Cabanne, Pierre	Van Gogh	Thames & Hudson	1969
Cherry, Bridget & Pevsner, Nikolaus	London 2: South	Yale University Press	2002
Cherry, Bridget & Pevsner, Nikolaus	London 3: North West	Penguin	1999
Cherry, Bridget & Pevsner, Nikolaus	London 4: North	Yale University Press	2002
Cherry, Bridget, O'Brien, Charles & Pevsner, Nikolaus	London 5: East	Yale University Press	2005
Clayton, Antony	Subterranean City	Historical Publications	2000
Dawson, Graham	'More on Bermondsey Floods – or Rather Stopping Them'	Surrey Archaeological Society	2013
Dixon, Ken	Effra: Lambeth's Underground River	The Brixton Society	2011
Fathers, David	The Regent's Canal	Frances Lincoln	2012
Fathers, David	The London Thames Path	Frances Lincoln	2015
Hampson, Tim	London's Riverside Pubs	New Holland	2011
Hyde, Ralph	The A to Z of Victorian London	Harry Margary	1987
Laxton, Paul	The A to Z of Regency London	Harry Margary	1985
Myers, Stephen	Walking on Water	Amberley Publishing	2011
Talling, Paul	London's Lost Rivers	Random House Books	2011
Sinclair, Iain	Swimming to Heaven: The Lost Rivers of London	The Swedenborg Society	2013
Sunderland, Septimus	Old London's Spas, Baths and Wells	John Bale, Sons & Danielsson Ltd	1915
—	Reference Atlas of Greater London	John Bartholomew & Sons	1961

THE OUTFALLS

Earl's Sluice	*River Fleet*	*River Tyburn*	*Hackney Brook*
River Walbrook	*River Neckinger*	*Falcon Creek*	*Counter's Creek*
River Effra	*Stamford Brook*	*River Westbourne*	

INDEX

Also by **David Fathers**

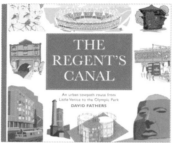

The Regent's Canal (2012)

The London Thames Path (2015)